Also Available from Eclipse Press

Affirmed and Alydar: Racing's Greatest Rivalry

At the Wire: Horse Racing's Greatest Moments, Updated Edition

Duel for the Crown: Affirmed, Alydar, and Racing's Greatest Rivalry

*The First Kentucky Derby: Thirteen Black Jockeys, One Shady Owner,
and the Little Red Horse That Wasn't Supposed to Win*

Great Horse Racing Mysteries: True Tales from the Track, Updated Edition

Kelso: Racing's Five-Time Horse of the Year

*The Kingmaker: How Northern Dancer Founded a Racing Dynasty,
Updated Edition*

Man o' War: Racehorse of the Century

*Ride of Their Lives: The Triumphs and Turmoil of
Racing's Top Jockeys, Updated Edition*

*The Seabiscuit Story: From the Pages of the Nation's
Most Prominent Racing Magazine*

Seattle Slew: Racing's First Undefeated Triple Crown Winner

*Secretariat: Racing's Greatest Triple Crown Winner,
50th Anniversary Edition*

Tales from the Triple Crown

The 10 Best Kentucky Derbies

War Admiral: Man o' War's Greatest Son

Women in Racing: In Their Own Words, Updated Edition

THOROUGHBRED
Legends®

*K*elso

Racing's Five-Time
Horse of the Year

S T E V E   H A S K I N

ECLIPSE
PRESS

Essex, Connecticut

ECLIPSE PRESS

An imprint of Globe Pequot, the trade division of
The Rowman & Littlefield Publishing Group, Inc.
4501 Forbes Blvd., Ste. 200
Lanham, MD 20706
www.rowman.com

Distributed by NATIONAL BOOK NETWORK

British Library Cataloguing in Publication Information available

Library of Congress Cataloging-in-Publication Data

The hardback edition of this book was previously cataloged as follows:

Name: Haskin, Steve, 1947-
Title: Kelso / by Steve Haskin.
Description: Lexington, KY: Eclipse Press ; Lanham, MD : National Book
   Network [distributor], 2003. | Includes index.
Identifiers: 2003102044 (print)
Subjects: Kelso (Race horse) | Race horses—United States—Biography.
Classification: SF355.K4 H27 2003 (print) | (DLC) 2003102044
LC record available at: https://lccn.loc.gov/2003102044

ISBN: 9781493080724 (paperback)
ISBN: 9781493080731 (electronic)
ISBN: 9781581501018 (cloth)

♾™ The paper used in this publication meets the minimum requirements
of American National Standard for Information Sciences—Permanence of
Paper for Printed Library Materials, ANSI/NISO Z39.48-1992.

KELSO

CONTENTS

Introduction...6
Where He Gallops, The Earth Sings
Chapter 1..12
A Classic Type Of Racehorse
Chapter 2..20
The Ugly Duckling
Chapter 3..34
Trainer Wanted/Horse For Sale
Chapter 4..48
Riding And Gliding
Chapter 5..56
A Legend Is Born
Chapter 6..76
The Master's Swan Song
Chapter 7..98
The Purple Gang
Chapter 8...120
Kelsoland
Chapter 9...126
The Times They Are A Changin'
Chapter 10..148
Long Live The King
Chapter 11..174
The End Of An Era
Epilogue..188
Final Farewell

Pedigree..198
Past Performances...199
Index...201
Photo Credits...206
About the Author..207

INTRODUCTION

Where He Gallops, The Earth Sings

"Once upon a time, there was a horse named Kelso
— but only once."
—*Daily Racing Form/Morning Telegraph*
columnist Joe Hirsch

T here have been many "once upon a times" since the great Kelso ruled the Sport of Kings from 1960 to 1964. But the great gelding's unprecedented five-year reign, known as "the Era of Kelso," gives his story a more epochal quality.

It was a period of transition for America. The stark images of World War II had all but faded. The mid-fifties had brought an age of innocence that would be remembered more as a state of mind than a chapter in the annals of America. The most controversial issue was how the movement of Elvis Presley's hips was corrupting teenage girls. As the sixties began, no one could possibly foresee the ominous events that lay just ahead.

Words like assassination, cult murder, LSD, overdose, hippy, protest riots, and Vietnam had no meaning to the blissful masses who were about to be led into Camelot by a young, vibrant pied piper they called JFK. Other than the Cold War always looming in the background, there was no reason to believe these halcyon days would not go on forever.

At the time, horse racing, along with baseball and boxing, was the most popular sport in the United States. Teams such as the New York Yankees, Green Bay Packers, and Boston Celtics built remarkable dynasties, but Kelso was the most remarkable ruler of them all. In each of the five consecutive years he was voted Horse of the Year, the New York Yankees made it to the World Series. But even the mighty Yanks managed to win only two championships during that time.

For five years Kelso came to embody all the qualities Americans looked for in their heroes. He was the underdog who captured a throne; the runt who would be king. And from his throne he ruled longer than any

other equine monarch in history. His earning five consecutive Horse of the Year titles is a feat beyond com-
prehension, as is his winning five consecutive runnings
in the two-mile Jockey Club Gold Cup.

And no single athlete was ever as dominant in New
York as was Kelso. Kelso's name seemed to leap off the
pages of New York City's newspapers every weekend.
Fans flocked to Belmont Park and Aqueduct in droves,
with Saturday crowds of more than 50,000 common-
place. And most of them came to see Kelso.

There was no American athlete at the time more
dependable than the resilient Kelso. It was as if trainer
Carl Hanford would wind him up and send him out for
one machine-like performance after another, a dozen
or so times every year for six years. From August 3,
1960 until November 11, 1963, Kelso made thirty-nine
starts, winning twenty-eight, while finishing in the top
three in thirty-six of them, with two fourths. And carrying heavy weight became the norm for him. He
made twenty-four starts carrying 130 pounds or more,
finishing in the money in nineteen of them.

Each year new foes would emerge to attempt to
overthrow him, but all failed. As the years passed and

the king began to age, he still refused to surrender his crown to the brash, youthful rivals who kept challenging his supremacy.

He faced his sternest test at age seven when the brilliant Gun Bow made a gallant, but futile, effort to dethrone him. When Kelso defeated Gun Bow in the 1964 Aqueduct Handicap before a massive Labor Day crowd, the roar that resounded from the grandstand was described by *Daily Racing Form/Morning Telegraph* columnist Charles Hatton as "The Niagara of sound."

Kelso was so revered that a party was thrown in his honor at Toot Shor's, New York City's most famous watering hole, which was the number one haunt for celebrities and athletes. As the end of Kelso's career neared, one fan at Aqueduct was overheard saying, "It just won't seem like Saturday without Kelso." People could not believe there ever would come a day when they no longer would see Kelso parading to the post, sporting a yellow ribbon tied to his forelock.

What made Kelso such a beloved hero to so many people, young and old? Maybe it was just plain old charisma? Noted racing writer David Alexander may have said it best for everyone: "If asked to state the reasons why Kelso was the greatest racehorse we have ever known, I'd simply tell you that I think he's done more things better on more occasions over a longer period of time than any other horse in history. Or maybe I'd say it's just that I love him."

When Kelso's racing days finally ended in early 1966, a book containing articles and facts about Kelso was published by owner Allaire du Pont's Woodstock Farm, with proceeds going to the University of Pennsylvania's School of Veterinary Medicine at New Bolton Center and the Grayson-Jockey Club Research Foundation. The title given to Mrs. du Pont's introduction said it all: "Where He Gallops, The Earth Sings" (also the epitaph on his gravestone).

Mrs. du Pont never thought of herself as the owner of Kelso, as one would own a possession. "How can anyone actually possess the courage and generosity of another living creature?" she once wrote of Kelso. "What we were able to do for Kelso was nothing compared with what he did for us. He was born with a will to win that never for a second deserted him. Kelso's story has a beginning, but it has no end, for I know his name will remain ever green as long as

there are horses and people who love them."

Steve Haskin
Hamilton Square, New Jersey, 2003

A Classic Type Of Racehorse

K elso had to be destined for greatness. There is no other way to explain how a horse deemed so undesirable as a youngster could become one of the most beloved horses of all time. It may have been easy to fall in love with Kelso the racehorse, but the same couldn't be said about the scrawny bay colt that was born on April 4, 1957, at Claiborne Farm in Paris, Kentucky. Not only was the son of Your Host and Maid of Flight nothing to look at, but he also had a nasty streak that eventually would put many exercise riders on the seat of their pants.

But Allaire du Pont was not thinking about temperament when she bred Maid of Flight to Your Host. She was just looking to breed a classic type of racehorse that could excel at distances at a mile and a quarter and farther. With Your Host's classy English bloodlines through his grandsires, Epsom Derby winners Hyperion and Mahmoud, and Maid of Flight's classy American bloodlines through Count Fleet and Man o' War, she felt such an outcross, or an absence of inbreeding, was the best way to accomplish this. This formula of crossing American and European bloodlines had proved successful with legendary breeders such as James R. Keene and Colonel E.R. Bradley.

Maid of Flight was a daughter of 1943 Triple Crown winner Count Fleet and a granddaughter of the legendary Man o' War.

Maid of Flight's dam, Maidoduntreath, was the result of a gift from Man o' War's owner Samuel Riddle to Mrs. Silas Mason, who, with her husband, operated Duntreath Farm in Lexington, Kentucky. Soon after Silas Mason died, Riddle presented Mrs. Mason with a season to Man o' War. She bred her mare Mid Victorian to the great stallion, and in the spring of 1939, Mid Victorian gave birth to Maidoduntreath, named in honor of Mrs. Mason's farm. Maidoduntreath never raced but became a decent broodmare. In addition to Maid of Flight, she produced 1950 Hollywood Oaks winner Mrs. Fuddy and other stakes winners Six

Fifteen and Scotch.

Sold as a yearling for $9,200, Maid of Flight raced twice for her new owner, James Edwards, before being acquired by Mrs. du Pont. She was a useful filly for Mrs. du Pont, placing in the Margate Handicap and Jeanne d'Arc Stakes at two. Sidelined by an injury as a three-year-old, she returned to race several times at four, placing in the Philadelphia Turf Handicap before her retirement.

Mrs. du Pont once described Kelso's pedigree as one part science, two parts her confidence in Your Host. Not only did Your Host have a royal pedigree but also courage in abundance. That the horse was still alive, much less able to breed mares, was remarkable considering all he'd been through.

In the spring of 1950, Your Host basked in the Kentucky Derby spotlight. Purchased for $20,000 by William Goetz from his father-in-law, Louis B. Mayer, who ran MGM Studios, Your Host captured the Del Mar Futurity and California Breeders' Champion Stakes at two. After victories the following spring in the San Felipe and Santa Anita Derby, he became the early favorite for the Kentucky Derby. Mayer called him the best horse he had ever bred.

Goetz hired longtime Del Mar public relations man Eddie Read to handle Your Host's publicity, and when the colt shipped to Kentucky in a railroad car, he did it with an unprecedented flair. Hanging from the car were banners that read: "Kentucky Bound, Derby Winner, 1950."

When Your Host romped by six and a half lengths in a seven-furlong allowance race at Keeneland, his reputation grew, and he was sent off as the 8-5 favorite in the Derby. With Johnny Longden aboard, he set the pace for the first mile, and then tired badly to finish ninth. After the Derby he rattled off five more stakes victories and concluded the year with eight wins in twelve starts and earnings of $253,375.

On New Year's Day, 1951, he began his four-year-old campaign by finishing second in the San Carlos Handicap to Bolero in a world-record time of 1:21. Five days later he carried 130 pounds to victory in the Santa Catalina Handicap. The following week he was back again in the San Pasqual Handicap. When Renown lugged in suddenly after turning for home, Your Host clipped his heels and fell to the ground, fracturing his ulna, which is located in the upper foreleg, right under the shoulder bone.

Veterinarians at the scene disagreed whether the horse should be euthanized. As he was insured by Lloyd's of London, the decision was made to try to save him because of his regal pedigree. By the Hyperion stallion Alibhai out of the great producer Boudoir II, by Epsom Derby winner and top sire Mahmoud, Your Host certainly was worth something as a stallion. Because of the extent of the fracture, veterinarians felt reconstructing the bones would be fruitless, so they decided to let nature heal the leg. Relying on the horse's courage and will to survive, the veterinarians used therapeutic rays and massages as the only treatments. All the while, a representative of the American Society for the Prevention of Cruelty to Animals (ASPCA) monitored every move.

Your Host was no stranger to misfortune. He had faced death as a weanling when he suffered a severe upper spinal injury that left him with a crook in his neck. Whenever he ran, he carried his head low and turned it slightly to one side.

Now, he was fighting for his life once again. Lloyd's

of London eventually paid off Goetz' $250,000 claim and took custody of the horse. It wasn't that they were anxious to own a broken-down horse, but when Mayer reminded them about the millions of dollars MGM paid them each year in insurance and threatened to cancel all its policies, Lloyd's had no choice but to pay Goetz and take control of the horse.

Veterinarians tried suspending Your Host from the rafters of his stall in a body sling to prevent him from putting weight on the damaged leg. When that failed, his stall was bedded down with sand and packed tightly around his body so he couldn't move. After several weeks of enduring constant pain, Your Host began to heal.

Agents for Lloyd's then sent Your Host to George W. Stratton's Circle S Ranch in Canoga Park, California, to complete his recovery. He had stood a short breeding season at Circle S when Humphrey S. Finney, president of Fasig-Tipton Sales Company, visited him. Finney admired Your Host's courage and secured a ninety-day option from Lloyd's to buy the horse for Fasig-Tipton at a price of $150,000.

Finney wanted to find a good home for Your Host,

but the highest price he was offered was $50,000. He told Your Host's amazing story to F. Wallis Armstrong, who had suffered from polio. Armstrong could relate to the crippling pain the horse had suffered and decided to buy him for the $150,000 asking price. Your Host was shipped to Armstrong's farm in New Jersey, where he stood for a $2,500 fee, with each share going for $7,500.

One spring morning in 1956, Dickie Jenkins, a former rodeo cowboy and Quarter Horse jockey, loaded Maid of Flight in a small van and drove her from Mrs. du Pont's farm near Middletown, Delaware, to Armstrong's Meadowview Farms in Moorestown, New Jersey, where she would be bred to Your Host. Mrs. du Pont had a few shares in Your Host, and his convenient location just up the turnpike made him a practical mate for Maid of Flight.

Jenkins had been working for Mrs. du Pont for four years when he arrived that spring morning at Meadowview Farms. He brought Maid of Flight off the van, then walked her to the breeding shed, where he held her securely as Your Host hobbled into the shed and mounted her. The nine-year-old stallion walked with a noticeable limp and was unable to bend his knee fully. His back legs controlled most of his movements. But the breeding went off without a hitch and soon Jenkins was trailering Maid of Flight back home.

He could have no way of knowing what a profound effect that mating would have on his life and the lives of so many others.

KELSO

CHAPTER 2

The Ugly Duckling

When Maid of Flight arrived at Claiborne Farm in Paris, Kentucky, to be bred to Ambiorix, the fact that she was in foal somehow slipped through the cracks. Thinking she was maiden mare (a mare who had never been bred), the farm personnel turned her out in a field with the other maiden mares. One day someone noticed that Maid of Flight was displaying signs of pregnancy. Claiborne's resident veterinarian, Colonel Floyd Sager, examined her and confirmed she was in foal. Believing he had discovered an unknown pregnancy, he had the farm deliver a note to Mrs. du Pont informing her that Maid of Flight was in foal. Having sent a letter along with the mare stating her condition, Mrs. du Pont understandably was incensed that Maid of Flight had been turned out with maiden mares.

Maid of Flight's foal was born without incident, and

no one at Claiborne really paid much attention to him, other than acknowledging Mrs. du Pont owned him. He had a narrow frame, bony hips, and each of his ribs could be counted. After first seeing the colt, Bull Hancock knew he'd have to use diplomacy when offering his opinion to Allaire du Pont, a longtime friend of the family.

Maid of Flight and her foal were turned out with the other mares and foals and seemed to adapt quickly. One afternoon in early May, Mrs. du Pont came to see the foal. Hancock had prepared her not to expect too much, but to Mrs. du Pont, looks were only a small part of a Thoroughbred's makeup. She firmly believed what was inside mattered most. If only she could have looked into her scrawny, little colt and seen his destiny, it surely would have reaffirmed her belief.

A few weeks after Mrs. du Pont's visit, Maid of Flight and her foal were put on a van and sent to Mrs. du Pont's Woodstock Farm, a 1,200-acre former cattle farm near Chesapeake City, Maryland. Mrs. du Pont and her husband, Richard, had purchased the tract along the Bohemia River shortly before Richard's death in 1943. The couple initially used the land mainly to raise their herd of Angus cows. It was virgin country then, perfect for Allaire's fox hunting.

At the time, Mrs. du Pont's racehorses were stabled at her farm near Middletown, Delaware, and trained over the adjacent track owned by longtime horseman Bayard Sharp. Not long before Kelso's birth, Mrs. du Pont moved her operation to Woodstock.

Dickie Jenkins had played a large part in the transformation of Woodstock from cattle farm to Thoroughbred farm. Jenkins and Mrs. du Pont discussed where the barns at Woodstock would be situated. He planted a number of the trees, put up the fencing, and hauled the old office to the farm on the back of a flatbed. Everything was painted yellow and gray, the colors of Bohemia Stable, the name under which Mrs. du Pont raced.

Jenkins was born in Jacksonville, Florida. As a youngster full of spit and vinegar, he began riding in Quarter Horse match races at the age of eight. He later joined the rodeo, riding broncs, and then became a Quarter Horse jockey before turning to jumpers. He described himself as a "wild little fella," who would ride anything with four legs and an attitude. No horse, no matter how ornery, was going to get the best of him. Jenkins, who was half Cherokee, also had an attitude, and the jock's room for him became a war zone. There he could settle any disputes with other riders without fear of retribution from the stewards.

If some rider shut him off during a race, he wouldn't say a word. Once in the privacy of the jock's room, however, he was free to "beat the dog s___"out of the rider. Sometimes, it took a rogue to handle a rogue, and Jenkins' reputation as someone who would ride any horse began to spread around the racetrack, as did his penchant for getting into scrapes.

Jenkins, who had spent two years driving a tank in an Army battalion known as "Hell on Wheels," once nearly beat a man to death in a bar fight. The man had hit him upside the head with a beer glass, leaving Jenkins' ear hanging by a thread and bouncing off his shoulder as he retaliated with a pool cue. Luckily, doctors were able to reattach Jenkins' ear.

In the early 1950s, Jenkins was riding for leading jump trainer Ray Woolfe. Woolfe recognized Jenkins' talents but warned him: "If you get into trouble one more time, I'm gonna fire you."

The night before he was to ride one of Woolfe's horses, Beaupre, at Belmont Park, Jenkins went to dinner at Luna restaurant, across the street from the track. Another jump rider, Joe Santo, was there with one of Jenkins' girlfriends. Despite Woolfe's warning, he and Santo began to mix it up.

The following morning Jenkins got to Woolfe's barn early to gallop Beaupre. The first thing he saw was Woolfe standing there glaring at him, with his hands on his hips. "Dickie Jenkins, I hate to do this, but if I had known about what happened earlier I would have scratched this horse. I'm gonna keep my word. As soon as you get off the horse after the race, you're fired."

So, Jenkins went back to his room after the race and packed his bag. He decided to catch a train home to Florida. Trainer Sid Watters tried to get him to stay, but Jenkins wanted out. "I ain't workin' for nobody," he told Watters. "I'm goin' home."

As he waited for a cab, a friend, Norman Cox, came driving by in his brand new Studebaker Golden Hawk. "Hey, what did you do, get fired?" he asked Jenkins, who told him the whole story. "Well, why don't you come with me down to Delaware? I'm workin' for Mrs.

du Pont at Bohemia Stables in Middletown, the old Chop Tank Farm. We need someone to break year-lings."

Jenkins figured he'd work there for a couple of weeks, get a few more bucks in his pocket, then head to Jacksonville. On April 3, 1953, he arrived at the farm and met Mrs. du Pont and farm manager Jimmy Hallahan. He also knew some of the other workers, Bobby Morris and Skeets Lambert. He spent two months breaking yearlings and said, "I gotta get outta here." But Mrs. du Pont was short of help and needed him. So, instead of staying a few weeks, he wound up staying sixteen years. For seven of those years, Jenkins and Kelso were inseparable. Jenkins exercised Kelso almost every time the horse went on the track, vanned him to every one of his races, and took him to the gate on the pony for all his races.

Spending so many hours a day with the horse and traveling so many miles ultimately cost him his mar-riage. With a horse like Kelso, he knew his responsibil-ities. For Jenkins that meant feeding, sending the tack out, helping out with the grooming, in addition to his regular job as exercise rider. It also meant running back and forth to the farm while his wife was pregnant, and traveling at inconvenient times. Eventually his wife left. It wasn't until he parted company with Kelso years later that Jenkins was able to return to a normal life.

Mrs. du Pont had wasted no time in coming up with a name for Maid of Flight's colt. With the horse being by Your Host, she immediately thought of her close friend, Mrs. Kelso Everett. The wife of Charles Everett, a prominent social figure from Wilmington, Delaware, Kelso Everett was "the most perfect hostess" Mrs. du Pont had ever known. Because she had always wanted to name a horse after her, Mrs. du Pont naturally was hoping Maid of Flight's first foal by Your Host would be a filly. Although she didn't get her wish, the name was too good to pass up. So, here was this ugly duckling that was born a colt, yet named after a woman, only to wind up a gelding.

Beneath the brown-paper wrapping were signs of what was to come. Kelso had the beginnings of a strong shoulder and front end, and a good-sized girth, but he was so narrowly built and awkward that casual observers failed to notice his attributes. He also had a certain refinement. He moved gracefully with deer-like legs, and his muzzle was described as being "so refined, he can drink water from a cup."

One day, while he was out in the paddock, irrigation pipes were brought out to water the drought-ravaged fields. Kelso's halter got hung on one of the sprinklers and he suffered two cuts on one of his cheeks. The scars eventually turned into two white spots, which remained noticeable throughout his career and were a source of curiosity.

As Kelso grew older, he still was "ratty looking and meaner than hell," according to Dickie Jenkins. Jenkins said you could throw your hat at Kelso and it would hang on him anywhere. When it was time to be broken, Kelso proved a challenge for his handlers. He liked to bite and meant it. And when anyone got up on his back, he'd prop and wheel, dropping the rider within seconds. In other words, he was Dickie Jenkins' kind of horse.

At first Jenkins didn't sense anything out of the ordinary about the colt. Kelso didn't seem to have much substance and moved awkwardly as he plodded along. But once Kelso broke into a high gallop, Jenkins could feel the flow and power beneath him. He realized that perhaps a swan was lurking inside the ugly duckling.

Still, Kelso had a lot of strikes against him. He had a bad temperament, he was unappealing to look at, and he was a notorious cribber — a horse that bites down on a hard object with his upper teeth and sucks air into his lungs. Although cribbing doesn't affect a race-horse's performance, it is considered a nasty habit, and it is mandatory for sales companies to announce before the bidding that a horse is a cribber.

In addition, he had a testicle that interfered with his action. Veterinarian John Lee, who also trained for Mrs. du Pont, had no choice but to recommend that Kelso be gelded.

Lee had vivid memories of Maid of Flight, who had a terrible disposition, and once struck at Lee with her front leg with such force she tore his coat and pants right off his body. The sight of Kelso resurrected those images.

So, one summer morning in 1958, Kelso, not yet having seen his second birthday, was subjected to what writer Red Smith called, "the unkindest cut of all." Jenkins, as usual, was right there, holding the young

horse while veterinarian George Rosenberger per-
formed what was to become one of the most famous
castrations in racing history. When it was complete,
Jenkins took Kelso's testicles and flung them atop the
roof of the barn, an act that horse people considered
good luck. The old wives' tale says to leave them there
until nature disposes of them.

Whenever confronted about his decision to geld
what was to become one of the greatest horses in history, Lee always gave the same response: "The results
obtained speak for themselves."

Kelso was now a gelding, but his nasty disposition
remained intact. He still would prop and wheel and try
to drop whoever was on him — usually Jenkins.
Despite Kelso's antics, the old rodeo rider never once
hit the dirt.

But at the barn, the gelding had become more social
after being spoiled rotten by Mrs. du Pont, and he
enjoyed the company of his numerous canine buddies.
Thanks to Mrs. du Pont's pampering, he developed an
insatiable love for sugar and especially chocolate ice
cream.

When Kelso turned two, physical problems prevented him from starting racing until early September. He developed a stifle problem, and whenever he was brought out of his stall, he would stop dead in his tracks. To get him going again, his handler would back him up three or four steps and let him get the stifle straightened out. Internally, he wasn't much better, as he'd often come down with colic. Jenkins said he lost track of how many times Kelso had to be fed intravenously. "I must have held a zillion intravenous bottles during his life," he said.

When Kelso finally did debut, on September 4 at Atlantic City Race Course, his trainer thought so little of the horse, he didn't even go to saddle him. Sent off at 6-1, Kelso sliced his way between horses after turning for home and blew by the leaders inside the sixteenth pole to win by a length and a quarter, covering the six furlongs over a track labeled good in a pedestrian 1:13 4/5.

Kelso's jockey, John Block, and Block's older brother, Henry, also a jockey, felt the gelding stood a good chance of winning and put a pretty good wager on him. Block, a twenty-one-year-old contract rider for Mrs. du Pont, had been instrumental in breaking Kelso

and schooling him at the gate. He had seen enough of the horse and been on him enough to know he had talent.

Henry Block had ridden for Mrs. du Pont as well, and was aboard Maid of Flight for many of her races. When he told Mrs. du Pont he had a younger brother coming up, she said to bring him down to the farm. She wanted the then seventeen-year-old John to concentrate on fox hunting, but Henry had convinced him the money was in riding Thoroughbreds, so little by little they coaxed her into letting John ride races for her.

Mrs. du Pont became like a second mother to John. When his father suffered a heart attack, Mrs. du Pont had her personal physician go see him. John stayed with Mrs. du Pont until his contract ran out in 1960 and then went to work for trainer Frankie Moore, who had a much larger stable. John retired from the saddle in 1969, and after a brief stint as a trainer, he, Henry, and another brother, Carl, who had been a jock's agent, opened a construction business in New Jersey, which they still operate.

Ten days after his first race, Kelso was back at Atlantic City for a six-furlong allowance race. He was bet down to 4-1, but this time he raced more evenly, closing a little in the final furlong to finish second to Dress Up. John Block blamed the loss on instructions not to hit the horse. Nine days later Lee sent Kelso back to Atlantic City for the third time in September. Entered in a seven-furlong allowance race over a faster, tighter surface, Kelso showed more speed than in his past two races. With veteran rider Walter Blum aboard this time, he battled head and head through rapid fractions of :22 and :44 2/5, only to give way at the end to Windy Sands, who beat him by three-quarters of a length.

After the race Lee noticed Kelso had rapped a tendon on his ankle. After returning home, he brought Kelso into the barn, took another good look at the ankle, and told Mrs. du Pont, "You ought to see if you can get rid of this horse, because he's gonna bow [his tendon] on you."

After hearing such an ominous prediction about a career-ending injury, Mrs. du Pont put Kelso up for sale. Her nephew, Gene Weymouth, offered to trade her his new cabin cruiser for Kelso, but she never entertained the bizarre offer.

Still, she decided to heed her trainer's advice and sell the horse. So began Mrs. du Pont's futile attempt to get rid of Kelso.

Trainer Wanted/Horse For Sale

D r. John Lee retired from training following Kelso's two-year-old campaign. Lee's veterinary practice in Philadelphia made it difficult for him to devote the necessary time to the Woodstock horses. And with Mrs. du Pont's stable growing in number, Lee suggested she find a full-time trainer.

When Carl Hanford, whose horses had been stabled across from Kelso at Atlantic City, heard the job was open, he immediately contacted Mrs. du Pont. The former jockey had watched Kelso train for his career debut, and although he felt Kelso was just an ordinary horse, he believed the gelding had a good chance against that particular field of maidens and bet a whopping five bucks on him at odds of 6-1.

Hanford didn't give Kelso a second thought until the following spring when he found out that Lee had retired and that Mrs. du Pont was looking for a trainer. He had known Mrs. du Pont for some time and immediately called her and applied for the job.

Although Frank Whiteley, who would one day train superstars Ruffian, Forego, and Damascus, was also being considered, Hanford thought he had a good chance of getting the job. He was training a string of horses in Florida at the time, and he contacted Mrs. du Pont, who asked him to come up to Maryland for an interview. Hanford was subsequently hired. Having worked with Mrs. du Pont's farm manager Jimmy Hallahan, who had rubbed horses for trainer "Irish Jimmy" Stewart the same time Hanford was there, certainly didn't hurt his chances of getting the job. Hanford was hired in February 1960 and quickly left Florida for Wilmington, Delaware.

Born on March 12, 1916, in Fairbury, Nebraska, Hanford was six when his family moved to Omaha. His father had died when Hanford was two, leaving his mother to take care of him and his seven brothers and three sisters. His only contact with horses took place when he visited his uncle's farm during the summer. His older brother, Bernard, known as Buddy, became a jockey and started riding for the legendary trainer Preston Burch. In 1933 Buddy was set to ride in his first Kentucky Derby when he was killed in a spill at Pimlico Race Course aboard a horse named Apprehensive. He was rushed to the hospital with what was believed to be a skull fracture, but died soon after arriving. He was twenty-one years old.

Buddy's death crushed the Hanford family, but it did not deter two of his brothers from following in his footsteps. Carl, in high school at the time, decided he also wanted to become a jockey. He began working with horses on weekends and after school at nearby Ak-Sar-Ben Racetrack. Like Buddy, he eventually went to work for Burch, walking hots and learning to gallop horses. After a short stint with Burch, he got a job with Charles "Tobe" Trotter and stayed with him for two years. It was Trotter who gave Hanford his first mounts.

Little did they know while stabled at the Empire City track in Yonkers, New York, in 1935, how close they would come to writing one of the great chapters in the history of the sport. It was there that Trotter took a liking to a two-year-old colt owned by Wheatley

Stable and trained by "Sunny" Jim Fitzsimmons. When Trotter found out the colt was for sale, he inquired about the price, but it was a bit beyond his means and he couldn't get the money together. The following year, the colt was sold to Charles Howard, and soon after, the name Seabiscuit grew into legend.

Hanford rode mostly in Maryland and Florida, after trying his luck in New England, but never found that one big horse or caught that one big break that would catapult him from obscurity to national recognition. One horse he rode was an exciting stretch runner named Brass Monkey, who became so popular on the New England circuit that he once appeared on stage at an awards dinner in Boston, taking the elevator up to the dining room.

Right behind Carl came his kid brother, Ira, whom everyone knew as "Babe." Babe followed Carl out of Nebraska, but instead headed to New York. Carl recommended he get a job with trainer Max Hirsch, who hired Babe and eventually began putting him on some of his better horses.

Babe won his first career race at Suffolk Downs, riding mostly for Hirsch's daughter, Mary, the first woman ever to get a trainer's license. After riding at Suffolk Downs through the summer and fall of 1935, Babe headed to Florida, where he was the leading rider at Hialeah as an apprentice. While at Hialeah, he occasionally traveled to Columbia, South Carolina, where Max Hirsch had a string of horses, including Bold Venture, who was not the soundest horse but had enormous potential. In the spring of 1936, Babe made the trip up to Columbia just to work the three-year-old. Hirsch ran Bold Venture one time in an allowance race in New York, then, in a bold move, sent him to Churchill Downs for the Kentucky Derby and named Babe to ride.

Racing eighth after a half-mile, Babe made a strong move with Bold Venture, putting him on the lead heading into the far turn. He held on the rest of the way, turning back the challenge of the 4-5 favorite, Brevity, to win by a head. Bold Venture went on to win the Preakness, but Babe couldn't ride him, having been suspended for a bumping incident with Granville, who had lost his rider soon after the start in the Derby. Bold Venture bowed a tendon after the Preakness and never ran again. At stud he sired two Kentucky Derby winners for Max Hirsch: Assault and Middleground.

While Babe's riding career was going well, Carl was being forced to change his own. By 1938 he had become too heavy to be a jockey. He galloped horses for "Irish Jimmy" Stewart for a while, and then got his trainer's license and began a small stable, putting Babe up on a number of his horses.

In 1941 Carl Hanford joined the Army, spending the war years at Fort Robinson in Nebraska with the remount service. Fort Robinson became home to some twenty thousand Thoroughbreds and mules. The mules were trained as pack animals, and Hanford and a number of other racetrackers worked with the Thoroughbreds, breaking and training them.

After being discharged from the Army following the war, Hanford returned to the racetrack and bought three cheap horses from a man in Lima, Ohio. He shipped the horses by boxcar to Delaware Park, and although two of them couldn't run a lick, one, named Legal Eagle, managed to win several races. Hanford then went to Florida and bought two horses, Jupiter Light and Whiffletree, both of whom would be successful, winning several races and beating stakes horses in allowance company. Jupiter Light won five of her first six starts, then after placing in the Fairy Chant Handicap finished third in the prestigious Beldame Stakes.

Hanford's main client was J.U. Gratton, who ran the lottery in Canada. Gratton was a heavy bettor and also played the stock market. When Hanford refused to tout Gratton on which horses to bet, Gratton fired him. Hanford soon rebuilt his stable, training for Art Rooney, longtime owner of the National Football League's Pittsburgh Steelers. In 1952 Carl had his first real star, La Corredora, whom Babe rode to many big wins, including the Monmouth Oaks and Ladies Handicap. Babe was nearing the end of his career, and he told Carl he would quit as soon as La Corredora was finished racing. He kept his word. In 1954 La Corredora retired, and so did Babe.

When Mrs. du Pont hired Carl, he turned all his horses over to Babe to train. Babe went on to have a successful career as a trainer, saddling multiple stakes winners such as Creme dela Creme, Munden Point, and Rhubarb. Creme dela Creme captured the 1966 Jersey Derby and finished second to Buckpasser in the

Arlington Classic, in which Buckpasser broke the world record for the mile.

It wasn't exactly a dream stable that awaited Carl Hanford when he took over the Bohemia Stable horses of Mrs. du Pont in the winter of 1960. There were seven maiden fillies; two three-year-old geldings, Kelso and Alias, another son of Your Host; and Kelso's two-year-old half brother, Amaloft. Hanford had always had good success with fillies, and with seven maiden fillies, Mrs. du Pont could very well have been playing the percentages when she hired him.

When Hanford took over, Mrs. du Pont was still trying to sell Kelso, but no one was interested. The previous fall, before Hanford was hired, Dickie Jenkins went to the airport one afternoon to pick up trainers Sid Watters and Burley Parke, who were looking to buy some horses. He drove them to Woodstock, dropped them off in front of the barn, and then went inside to bring out the horses that were for sale — Kelso, a Turn-to colt, and a Cosmic Bomb colt. Of the three, Kelso was the only one who had already run. Jenkins threw a halter on Kelso and led him out of the barn. As soon as he walked out, Burley Parke said, "You can put him back in." Without even stopping, Jenkins turned around and took Kelso back in the barn. Parke wound up buying the Turn-to colt, while Watters took the Cosmic Bomb.

That was only one example of the lack of interest in Kelso. One afternoon in the fall of 1959, a bloodstock agent approached John Nerud, who had trained a number of top horses, including 1957 Belmont Stakes winner Gallant Man.

"I know of a nice two-year-old that Mrs. du Pont is looking to sell for forty thousand," he told Nerud. "His name is Kelso."

Standing next to Nerud was trainer Jack Weipert. "You don't want that horse," he said to Nerud. "He's gettin' ready to bow."

Nerud backed off and started to make some inquiries about Kelso. When he asked someone else about the horse, he was told, "Forget it, he's a cribber and a stall walker." That was enough for Nerud. Between Kelso's having those two bad habits and an uncertain tendon, Nerud turned down the offer.

It had become apparent that Kelso was unwanted goods. Some of the country's top trainers, all with a

keen eye for a horse, had rejected him. It was like trying to get rid of the runt of the litter, one with so many
bad physical and mental traits, warning sirens went off
the second someone laid eyes on him.

The spring of 1960 saw the Triple Crown come and
go without establishing a leader. The two highly tout-
ed three-year-olds, Tompion and Bally Ache, both fell
to the 6-1 Venetian Way in the Kentucky Derby, with
Bill Hartack aboard. Bally Ache rebounded to win the
Preakness by four lengths, as Venetian Way beat only
one horse in the six-horse field. In the Belmont, Celtic
Ash, who had finished third in the Preakness at 7-1,
came from last with a powerful run to win easily by
five and a half lengths under Hartack, with Venetian
Way, now ridden by Eddie Arcaro, second and
Tompion fourth. It was a division in chaos.

Meanwhile, a million miles from the Triple Crown
scene, Mrs. du Pont still had Kelso for sale. Most of the
riders on the farm wanted nothing to do with him out
of fear. But Jenkins had no problem handling Kelso
and began to like what he was feeling beneath him.
That spring the stable had moved from the farm to
Delaware Park. Orville Mahoney was brought in by

Hanford to work the horses, and he got on Kelso several times. On other occasions Jenkins would drive the twenty-five miles from the farm to the track to gallop and work the gelding. Because of Kelso's antics of wheeling in circles and attempting to throw his riders, he was equipped with a "running martingale" with special rings on the bit to prevent him from tangling his reins when he wheeled. The martingale is a piece of equipment that stabilizes a horse's head and helps the rider maintain better control.

One morning, with Kelso nearing his first start of the year, Hanford sent the horse out for a five-furlong work. The Delaware track was very deep, and works of 1:02 and 1:03 were considered fast. Kelso hauled Jenkins around there in :59 and change. When they returned to the barn, Jenkins told Hanford, "I had this horse's mouth wide open and was standing up on him."

Jenkins spotted his friend, Johnny Knowles, who had just driven from the farm to deliver bales of hay. "We got a damn good horse here," Jenkins told him. "This son of a gun can fly."

"Who's that?" Knowles asked.

"Kelso," Jenkins said. "I worked him this morning

and he went in :59 and some change, and I didn't do nothin' but sit there folded up on him."

The way Jenkins described Kelso, it was like "sitting on a panel fence" when he got up on the horse. But once Kelso started getting into stride, he felt like "a stick of dynamite ready to blow up. Every time he changed leads and picked it up, it was like sitting on a new, fresh horse."

Hanford had also spotted something in Kelso soon after taking over his training. He told his veterinarian, Alex Harthill, who traveled each spring to Delaware from his home in Kentucky, "Doc, I got a horse you won't believe. He's the runningest horse I've ever been around."

Harthill, who also remembered Kelso's being for sale for as low as $25,000, thought, "Sure, I hear that all the time." He would soon find out just how right Hanford was.

Around the same time, Mrs. du Pont was looking to buy a filly from Bull Hancock, who had two for sale in New York. She sent Hanford to look at the two fillies before finalizing any deal. Hanford drove up and gave the okay on one of them, a filly named Venice. When he called Mrs. du Pont, she told him, "I've got good news. I just got an offer for Kelso, and I think we might be able to sell him."

Hanford advised her against it. "Don't sell this horse," he said. "The way he's been working, he might be any kind. And with seven fillies, we won't have any balance in the stable."

Hanford also felt Mrs. du Pont's asking price was way too low. He had been unable to find a race at Delaware Park for Kelso but had him lined up for a non-winners of two allowance race at Monmouth Park on June 22. He knew his former client Art Rooney would be interested in the horse. "If this horse doesn't win, I guarantee you I'll be able to sell him for $25,000," Hanford told her.

So, with the three-year-old division in complete confusion, Kelso headed to battle for the first time that year. Surely no one even remotely regarded him as being in the same class as horses like Tompion and Venetian Way. But regardless of his many flaws, Kelso already was a winner and hadn't finished worse than second in three starts. He never would bow that tendon. And he never again would devote his waking

hours to dumping his riders. And he never again would be called ratty looking. And he never again would be for sale.

Riding And Gliding

Allaire Crozer du Pont loved horses as far back as she could remember. She acquired the passion from her mother's father, Edward S. Beal, who was an expert fox hunter and member of the Radnor Hunt Club. He would often mount up and tell his grand-daughter, "Come on, child, you get on and follow."

Allaire's father was a partner in the stock brokerage firm Stroud & Company in her hometown of Philadelphia, and she attended the exclusive Oldfield School in Glencoe, Maryland. But as she sat through her classes, horses preoccupied her mind.

Allaire spent much of her leisure time riding and eventually began competing in equine junior miss classes and at horse shows. As a young adult, she became a mistress of foxhounds of a hunt club on Maryland's Eastern Shore.

It was this love of horses that would one day manifest itself in the form of Woodstock Farm, where horses were pampered and provided with the best of everything. Horses encompassed her world, just as they would her daughter, Lana, who became a top-class equestrienne and three-day-event rider. At the 1964 Tokyo Olympics, Lana won a silver medal as a member of the U.S. Three-Day Event Team, just months before Kelso nailed down his fifth straight Horse of the Year title with his victory in the Washington, D.C., International. Lana, the first female Olympic eventer, won her medal riding her mother's retired Thoroughbred, Mr. Wister.

Allaire Crozer's appreciation for the speed and grace of the horse also attracted her to flying. She had always relished the freedom that riding horses gave her. The wind blowing in her face and the feeling of soaring above the rolling green hills were her life's elixir. Piloting gliders elicited those same sensations.

While attending Oldfield School, Allaire met her roommate's brother, Richard C. du Pont, part of the long line of descendants of Eleuthere Irenee (E.I.) du Pont, who founded the du Pont Company in

Wilmington, Delaware, in 1802. The company began by manufacturing gunpowder and eventually grew into a world-renowned science-based chemical company after being purchased by three du Pont cousins a century later.

Bound by their mutual love of flying, Allaire and Richard married several years later. He had been flying gliders since high school and had founded the Campus Soaring Club as a freshman at the University of Virginia. In 1932 he transferred to the Curtiss-Wright Technical Institute. The following year, Richard flew the first Senior Albatross glider at the U.S. National Soaring Championships held in Elmira, New York. On September 21 of that year, he set the American sailplane distance record by flying 121.6 miles.

On June 25, 1934, he flew within two miles of New York City from Elmira and established a new world distance record of 158 miles. Five days later he set the U.S. altitude record for sailplanes by climbing to 6,223 feet.

Richard was named the U.S. Soaring Champion in 1934, 1935, and 1937, and was posthumously inducted into the U.S. Soaring Hall of Fame in 1954.

Richard was not content with holding many of the soaring records unless he could share the honors with Allaire. So, with Richard's help, Allaire set out to establish new soaring records for women. Taking off from Elmira, he would fly his plane above hers, passing sandwiches to her, tied to a long rope. Allaire wound up setting records for both distance and altitude.

When World War II broke out, Richard became invaluable as a glider pilot and was awarded the Distinguished Service Cross for leading a glider landing in Sicily. In 1943 he was killed at age thirty-two while testing a new glider for the Army. Allaire continued to fly, never considering giving it up after her husband's death.

She eventually built a landing strip on Woodstock Farm and often chartered planes to fly to the racetrack to watch Kelso run.

Allaire du Pont introduced her Bohemia Stable silks to racing in 1942, purchasing a filly from J.O. Keene (who lent his name to Keeneland racetrack) named Panamerica, who would become the dam of Mr. Wister, the future Olympian. With the assistance of her friend, A.B. "Bull" Hancock of Claiborne Farm, she acquired additional bloodstock.

She also purchased additional land near Middletown, Delaware, where she would stable her horses, using the adjacent training track owned by Bayard Sharp. It wasn't until 1956, the year before Kelso's birth, that she had her first good horse, a New Jersey-bred colt named Ambehaving, who captured a series of state-bred races before winning the Remsen Stakes at Aqueduct.

In the late fifties she moved her Thoroughbred operation to Woodstock Farm. Soon, fields of Kentucky bluegrass and timothy clover, rows of evergreen trees, and miles of white three-plank fencing adorned the farm's rolling hills.

Mrs. du Pont was closely involved with the running of Woodstock Farm, with help from her loyal staff, including farm manager Jimmy Hallahan and Dickie Jenkins. Despite her wealth and social status, she made her employees feel at home and treated them as if they were family, often inviting them to parties. And she wasn't averse to going against the grain in the finest tradition of *The Prince and the Pauper*. In keeping with her adventurous spirit but not necessarily her refined public image, Mrs. du Pont would often let Dickie Jenkins take the wheel, knowing he drove without a license and with the same passion for speed he had on the racetrack. One night Jenkins was going well over the speed limit when the pair spotted a roadblock ahead. They looked at each other and knew immediately they had to switch seats. With Jenkins still behind the wheel, Mrs. du Pont managed to slide over him to change places.

On another occasion they were driving back to Maryland from Aqueduct when Mrs. du Pont said, "Dickie, I'm starving, do you have any money?"

Jenkins told her he was broke. They pulled in to a rest stop on the New Jersey Turnpike and bought a bag of caramel corn with their last few pennies, leaving them with nothing for tolls. When they pulled up to the tollbooth, Mrs. du Pont told the attendant who she was and that she had run out of cash, and he let them through.

And then there was the other side of Mrs. du Pont that most everyone saw. In 1961 she was at Saratoga to accept the plaque commemorating Kelso as Horse of the Year. She rose to speak, and with an endearing shyness and humility, expressed her pride and gratitude in her usual articulate manner. As she returned to her seat, one normally cynical Turf writer turned to the person next to him and said, "Class...sheer class!"

But before Mrs. du Pont became a racing ambassador of sorts through Kelso, she was doing her part to strengthen the Thoroughbred industry in Maryland. As Woodstock Farm was converted into a Thoroughbred operation, the number of Thoroughbred farms in the area began to increase. One notable addition was Windfields Farm, owned by Edward P. Taylor, who also owned a large breeding farm of the same name in Canada.

During an earlier visit from Taylor and his wife, Mrs. du Pont had encouraged Taylor to build a farm in Maryland. The land across the road from Woodstock's main gate was for sale and Taylor decided to buy it, eventually adding some acreage that Mrs. du Pont owned. Not long after, he would breed and race Northern Dancer, who would win the 1964 Kentucky Derby and Preakness. Northern Dancer would stand at stud at Windfields and go on to make Thoroughbred breeding history there.

Mrs. du Pont would see one of her own horses make history of a different sort as Kelso geared up for the major fall stakes of 1960. The world's highest flying female glider pilot would soon be soaring higher than she'd ever soared before.

KELSO

CHAPTER 5

A Legend Is Born

By October of 1960, Kelso had developed into a top-quality horse — far beyond the expectations of Carl Hanford and Mrs. du Pont. He had rattled off four straight stakes scores and had won six of his seven starts as a three-year-old, his only defeat coming in the Arlington Classic. Suddenly, the ugly duckling wasn't so ugly any more. The grace and elegance that lay hidden for so long were now surfacing in all their splendor. "Kelly," as Mrs. du Pont began calling him, was growing and filling out and, in short, was turning into a class racehorse. While he still was not going to threaten anyone in beauty contests, his artistry emerged once the gates opened and he was able to reach out and glide effortlessly with those magnificent, fluid strides.

With all of Kelso's victories having come in New York and New Jersey, Hanford decided to return to

Chicago for the prestigious Hawthorne Gold Cup, where Kelso would be taking on top-class older horses for the first time. This race would prove whether Kelso was merely a good, classy three-year-old, or a potential threat for Horse of the Year honors.

His three-year-old season had started off in exciting fashion. When Hanford was unable to find a race for Kelso at Delaware Park, he shipped him to Monmouth Park for a six-furlong allowance race on June 22. Bill Hartack, who had won the Kentucky Derby on Venetian Way and the Belmont aboard Celtic Ash, was riding at Monmouth. Hanford called Hartack's agent, known only as "Scratch Sheet," and told him about the nice three-year-old eligible for a non-winners of two, and asked whether Hartack would like to ride him. Hartack took the mount and hopped aboard Kelso for the gelding's three-year-old debut. Sent off as the even-money favorite in the eight-horse field, Kelso blew everyone away — his connections and his opposition — winning by ten lengths in a sharp 1:10, as Hartack drove him hard to the wire to give him the necessary seasoning. There would be no more talk about selling the horse.

On July 16 Kelso made his first trip to New York,

stretching out in a one-mile allowance race at Aqueduct. This time, Walter Blum, who had ridden Kelso in the gelding's third start at two, was given the mount. Blum thought little of Kelso when he rode him the first time, and Hanford wanted to make sure he realized he was on a totally different animal this time.

"Make sure you're tied on to this guy leaving the gate," Hanford told Blum in the saddling area. "He's so ready and raring to go he's gonna pull you to the lead, and that's the way he's gonna win."

Kelso proved his Monmouth victory was no fluke, as he shot to the lead and won wire to wire by twelve lengths. His time of 1:34 1/5 was only three-fifths of a second off the track record, and even though Aqueduct had just opened the year before and track records were falling constantly, that still was quick for an allowance horse. No other three-year-old in New York had ever run a faster mile. Blum would never again ride Kelso, but it certainly wasn't the last he'd ever see of him. Ironically, Blum would become the rider of Kelso's greatest rival, Gun Bow.

This was a great time for New York racing. Aqueduct, located just off the Belt Parkway and a short distance from Jamaica Bay, was being called the racetrack of the future. It was spacious and colorful, and most important, it had its own subway stop. New Yorkers fell in love with it and flocked there by train, bus, and automobile. It quickly became known as "The Big A." On Memorial Day, 1960, a record 70,992 fans showed up to see Bald Eagle win the Metropolitan Handicap. And, yes, he set a new track record of 1:33 3/5.

Racing's new magical kingdom needed a king, and although no one knew it at the time, a new reign had begun on July 16. Kelso would go on to win his first nine starts at Aqueduct and ended his career with a record of twenty victories from twenty-seven starts at The Big A, with most of the defeats coming late in his career.

After his brilliant triumph at Aqueduct, Kelso was ready for his stakes debut. Hanford decided to run him right back a week later, shipping him to Chicago for the Arlington Classic. Babe Hanford was taking time off from training and was working at Arlington as a patrol judge. Carl called and asked him to suggest a local rider. Babe told him to try Steve Brooks, a veteran jockey who had won the 1949 Kentucky Derby aboard Calumet Farm's Ponder. Prior to that, Brooks had ridden many of Calumet's other great horses. He was the regular rider for Coaltown and also for Citation after the Triple Crown winner returned to the races as a five-year-old following a thirteen-month layoff.

Hanford gave Brooks the mount on Kelso for the Arlington Classic, a one-mile race run out of the chute. Kelso, who was sent off as the second choice behind Derby winner Venetian Way, broke slowly and found himself behind a wall of horses. Brooks was never able to get him free, and Kelso ran bottled up the entire way, finishing a lackluster eighth, beaten seven and a half lengths by winner T. V. Lark. After returning, Brooks was visibly upset at the turn of events. "I can't even tell you what kind of horse you have," he told Hanford. "I couldn't let him run a yard at any point in the race."

Kelso was so fresh after the race and feeling so full of himself, they could hardly cool him out. Hanford felt he'd better run him back right away. The mile and one-sixteenth Choice Stakes at Monmouth was coming up in ten days, and Hanford felt that would be a perfect spot to bring him back.

After his bad defeat in Chicago, Kelso was sent off as the 7-2 third choice behind the co-favorites, Count

Amber and John William. Count Amber was coming off an impressive four and a half-length victory in an Aqueduct allowance race, in which he covered the mile in 1:34 4/5. John William was a veteran stakes performer who had won the Gotham and Withers stakes and finished second in the Santa Anita Derby and Arlington Classic. Also coming off an impressive allowance win at Aqueduct was Careless John, who had Walter Blum aboard.

The Choice turned out to be a stroll in the park for Kelso, who, under Hartack, tracked the early pace, and then drew off to win by seven lengths. His time of 1:41 1/5 for the mile and one-sixteenth was only a fifth of a second off the track record. People were now becoming aware of Mrs. du Pont's gelding as he headed back up to New York for a series of three-year-old stakes.

He wasn't ready for the mile and a quarter Travers Stakes at Saratoga, which went to Tompion, who romped by six lengths, with Hartack aboard for the first time. The Travers completed quite a triple for Hartack, who captured the Kentucky Derby, Belmont Stakes, and Travers that year with three different horses.

When Hanford entered Kelso in the one-mile Jerome

Handicap at Aqueduct on September 3, he had no idea that Tompion would come right back off only two weeks rest. Hanford wanted to get Hartack to ride Kelso again, but Hartack was trying to keep the mount on Tompion. Hanford waited as long as he could, then finally told Scratch Sheet, "If you don't get back to me, I'm gonna put somebody else on this horse." When he still hadn't gotten any word from Scratch Sheet, he went after the legendary rider Eddie Arcaro, who was nearing the end of his illustrious career.

Hanford called Arcaro's agent, Bones LaBoyne, and asked him whether Arcaro was interested in riding Kelso in the Jerome. LeBoyne obviously had seen Kelso in the flesh. "Sure," he said. "We'll ride that little bale of wire."

Dickie Jenkins vanned Kelso up to Aqueduct for the Jerome and took him to the post on the pony. "What do you know about this horse?" Arcaro asked him. Jenkins couldn't believe "The Master" was asking him what he thought. "The only thing I can tell you is, when the man says go, just reach up there and take a hold of him. He'll run his own race."

Kelso was made the 5-2 second choice behind the 9-

5 Tompion, who was ridden by Larry Adams, who had gained the mount instead of Hartack. After the break, Four Lane and Udaipur cut out a wicked pace of :22 3/5 and :45 2/5, with Arcaro sitting chilly on Kelso in ninth, within striking range of Tompion, who was in fifth. When Arcaro asked Kelso to pick it up around the turn, he began passing horses one by one, including Tompion, who was going nowhere. Careless John, carrying 116 pounds to Kelso's 121, took the lead just inside the eighth pole and set sail for home. Arcaro had Kelso rolling on the far outside but still had almost three lengths to make up on Careless John. Although Careless John closed his final quarter in a sharp :24 2/5, he couldn't hold off the relentless charge of Kelso, who stuck his head in front just at the wire. The time for the mile was 1:34 4/5, a new stakes record.

Kelso came out of the Jerome in excellent shape. Arcaro was impressed with his new mount, and after the race he bought Dickie Jenkins a new set of tires for his car. Arcaro would not relinquish his seat on Kelso until the legendary rider concluded his career in America at the end of the 1961 season. He did ride briefly in Australia in the winter of 1962 before officially retiring from the saddle.

Hanford ran Kelso back eleven days later against three-year-olds in the Discovery Handicap. Careless John had returned for another crack at the gelding, as had Count Amber. This time Kelso was assigned 124 pounds, giving eight pounds to both horses.

At the start Kelso swerved and lost valuable position going into the first turn. But Arcaro settled him in fourth, about three lengths off the pace. Entering the stretch, Kelso had to steady behind horses, waiting for an opening. When Arcaro spotted a hint of daylight, he gunned Kelso through. Careless John was running another big race, but Kelso lowered his head and battled him through the final furlong, easing clear at the end to win by a length and a quarter in 1:48 2/5, a new track record for a mile and one-eighth.

Hanford didn't think Kelso was ready to tackle the top older horses in the country, such as Bald Eagle, Sword Dancer, and Dotted Swiss, in the Woodward Stakes. Instead, he stretched him out to a mile and five-eighths in the Lawrence Realization at Belmont Park, two weeks after the Discovery. Careless John, Tompion, and T. V. Lark all showed up for the Woodward, four days before the Lawrence Realization, and were given a good spanking by the older horses. Careless John ran well to finish fourth, beaten only four lengths by the victorious Sword Dancer, the defending Horse of the Year. But Tompion and T. V. Lark were never factors and were soundly beaten.

Oddly enough, Tompion came right back in the Lawrence Realization four days later against Kelso. It was the C.V. Whitney colt's sixteenth start of the year, and the long season had begun to take its toll. Kelso was made the 1-2 favorite, and he had no trouble, beating Tompion by four and a half lengths and equaling Man o' War's track record of 2:40 4/5.

Kelso had now won at five distances in 1960, from six furlongs to a mile and five-eighths, and he was riding a four-race winning streak. Finally, it was time to face older horses. With the two-mile Jockey Club Gold Cup still to be run at the end of October, victories in that race and in the mile and a quarter Hawthorne Gold Cup would put Kelso in the running for Horse of the Year honors. Just a year earlier Burley Parke had only needed a quick glance to tell this was a horse not even worth looking at.

In mid-October, Kelso boarded a plane to Chicago, accompanied by Dickie Jenkins and groom Billy Hall. After landing in Chicago, he was loaded on a van to Hawthorne. Also on the van, having taken a different flight, was Calumet's hard-knocking four-year-old On-and-On, who would be one of Kelso's main challengers in the Hawthorne Gold Cup. He had won the Brooklyn Handicap that year, along with four other stakes, and rarely finished off the board. A big bay colt by Nasrullah, On-and-On dwarfed Kelso.

"Look-a here, Bill," Jenkins said to Hall, as the horses stood side by side. "You'd think this big ol' horse would eat Kelso up. Man, look at the difference in them. Ol' On-and-On looks like a draft horse compared to him." Jenkins always said the gelding's narrow body made it look as though his front legs came from the same hole.

Hall, who was from Pittsville, on the Eastern Shore of Maryland, was Kelso's groom for the first three years of the gelding's career. When Lee assigned him the horse, Hall thought he was "just another horse named Joe." But as he worked with Kelso, he couldn't help but notice how intelligent and professional the gelding

was. Hall would often say that Kelso "had more horse sense than most men." The young horse never ate too much or too little. He always knew what he was supposed to do. As long as Hall fed Kelso carrots cut up in small pieces, the horse was happy.

When Hall and Jenkins arrived at Hawthorne, they had no idea what was in store. The conditions there were harsher than at the East Coast tracks. Sleeping in the tack room, they were forced to stay up most of the night because rats "the size of possums" were running around the room. Also during their stay, a man was found dead in his car on the backstretch. The day they arrived, the track veterinarian came to check Kelso and told them that in the previous day's first race someone had managed to stuff sponges up the nostrils of every horse in the race except the winner. Jenkins immediately arranged to have a security guard outside their barn.

Another of Kelso's main competitors in the Gold Cup was Mary Keim's tough three-year-old Heroshogala, who was making his twentieth start of the year for Chicago-born trainer Phil "P.G." Johnson. Heroshogala was coming off a pair of stakes victories at Hawthorne, and earlier had finished third in the

American Derby and fourth in the Arlington Classic.

Whenever Johnson ran a horse at Hawthorne, he would rent a room near the track. This time, however, all the rooms were booked. Babe Hanford, still a patrol judge there, offered to let Johnson use his motel room, which was only five minutes from the track. Johnson used Babe's room to shower and change, although the two never really saw much of each other or had much conversation. Babe was not known as a big talker and, in fact, had been nicknamed "The Clam."

One day, a week before the Hawthorne Gold Cup, Johnson was in the motel room going over the nominations and weights for the big race with Babe. He saw that Heroshogala was carrying 119, with Kelso at 117. Hawthorne racing secretary Frank "Pat" Farrell had his doubts about Kelso's ability and treated him kindly in the weights. Johnson was confident in his horse and really wasn't worried about Kelso, never having seen him run. All he knew was that Kelso had won a few three-year-old stakes in New York. Johnson showered, got dressed, and was tying his shoes when he heard Babe cackling at him. When he kept it up, Johnson finally said, "Okay, you're trying to tell me something.

What is it?"

"You're giving two pounds to my brother's horse," Babe reminded him.

"So, what?" Johnson replied.

"He's gonna beat you the length of the stretch," Babe said bluntly.

Johnson couldn't let that statement go unchallenged. "I know you're too cheap to bet, but if you want to bet something, I'll bet you horse for horse."

Babe accepted. "Okay, but I'm telling you, you got no chance to beat this horse."

Johnson took another look at the weights. He had no problem giving Kelso two pounds, and he felt On-and-On, who carried second high weight of 122 pounds, was beginning to tail off. It poured the night before the race, and Johnson knew his horse could handle the mud. The track was so deep, *Daily Racing Form* columnist Charles Hatton wrote that it "required some archeology to find the bottom." Because of Kelso's stifle problems, Hanford was always a bit wary of running him in deep going.

Having no desire to watch the race from the box with the owner, Johnson went up on the porch of the jockey's room. Just minutes before post time, a jock's agent known only as Ham Jam came running frantically out of the jock's room and sped past Johnson. He dashed down the stairs and headed for the hundred-dollar mutuel window. When he returned, now much calmer and walking at a normal pace, someone asked him, "Where the hell were you going?"

Ham Jam explained, "Arcaro gave me five thousand bucks to bet on his horse and I forgot about it. A bell went off in my head at the last minute." Fortunately for Ham Jam, Hawthorne had large-denomination betting windows, which were less crowded; otherwise, he would have been shut out. "I would have had to book the bet," he said, "and then I would have had to leave town."

Arcaro's bet shattered whatever confidence Johnson had in his horse's chances. After all, when a jockey like Eddie Arcaro bets five thousand dollars on a horse that has just won a few minor three-year-old stakes, it has to start you thinking. Luckily, the only bet Johnson had on the race was the one with Babe, and at that point there was nothing he could do about it.

The start was uneventful, and Arcaro had Kelso tucked in along the inside early on, steadying briefly. He

then moved past Heroshogala down the backstretch, and as they neared the top of the stretch, Arcaro gunned Kelso to the lead from the inside. Passing the eighth pole, the pair was already three lengths in front. With Arcaro sitting motionless, Kelso drew off to win eased up by six lengths in 2:02 over the muddy track. Heroshogala followed Kelso's path along the rail and just got up to beat out On-and-On for second.

After the race Heroshogala's owner, Mary Keim, felt Kelso had interfered with her horse and asked Johnson why there was no foul claim. Johnson told her, "The only foul was that we could have gotten pneumonia when that sonofabitch went by us." The following winter the relationship between Johnson and Keim ended.

Kelso had now demolished top-class three-year-olds and older horses, and he had a legitimate claim to the Horse of the Year title. His final test would come in the Jockey Club Gold Cup in two weeks. Standing in his way was Cain Hoy Stable's Bald Eagle, who was coupled with Tooth and Nail, a speed horse who was entered strictly as a pacesetter.

Bald Eagle had maintained his form all year, winning the Widener Handicap and Gulfstream Park

Handicap in the winter, the Metropolitan Handicap in the spring, and the Aqueduct Handicap in early September. After finishing third in the Woodward, he was put on the grass in the Man o' War Stakes by trainer Woody Stephens and finished second to longshot Harmonizing, while finishing ahead of Sword Dancer. Stephens felt a victory in the Jockey Club Gold Cup, followed by a win in the Washington, D.C., International at Laurel would be enough to nail down Horse of the Year honors.

Also in the Gold Cup was the Argentinean stayer, Don Poggio, who was coming off a three-length victory in the mile and a half Manhattan Handicap. Earlier, he had romped by almost six lengths in the mile and three-quarters Merchants' and Citizens' Handicap at Saratoga. The others given an outside chance were the Man o' War winner Harmonizing and Dotted Swiss.

On the morning of October 29, steam rose from the horses as they cooled out in the chilly air. Early heavy rains had turned the Belmont track sloppy, and when Mrs. du Pont went to check out the surface, she didn't like what she saw.

"This track looks terrible," she told Hanford. "Do

you think we should scratch him?"

"No, we shouldn't scratch him," Hanford told her. "He's gonna be the favorite, and he'll handle any kind of going."

Mrs. du Pont suggested asking Arcaro's opinion, but Hanford insisted Arcaro didn't know any more about the horse's ability to handle an off track than he, as trainer, did. Mrs. du Pont gave the okay to run.

The early stages of the Gold Cup often seem to be run in slow motion, with jockeys trying to restrain their mounts to save something for the end of the grueling two miles. But on this day, Alex Ycaza, on Tooth and Nail, had no visions of grandeur. He was on a suicide mission and he knew it. His job was to blast the race wide open early and possibly force Arcaro to move too soon, setting him up for Bald Eagle's big late run. But Arcaro didn't become one of the greatest riders of all time by falling for some rabbit-in-the-hat trick. He let Tooth and Nail open up a twelve-length lead after three-quarters. It actually was Sam Boulmetis on the stayer, Don Poggio, who went after Tooth and Nail first, with Arcaro content to follow close behind.

Don Poggio whittled away at Tooth and Nail's lead

and took over passing the half-mile pole. Kelso was sitting just off his flank, waiting to pounce. The two horses began to draw away from the rest, leaving Bald Eagle floundering in the slop. At the three-sixteenths pole, Kelso disposed of Don Poggio and drew off to win by three and a half lengths, with Don Poggio finishing ten lengths ahead of Bald Eagle. The previous record for the two miles was Sword Dancer's 3:22 1/5, set in the 1959 Gold Cup. Kelso, over a deep, sloppy track, ran his two miles in 3:19 2/5, a new American record.

There now was no question in Arcaro's mind he was riding something special. "He can beat anything at any distance from six furlongs to two miles," he said after dismounting. "At the half-mile pole, I said, 'I'm going to find out now if I have the best horse.' I sure did. Pulling up, I was breathing harder than Kelso."

Kelso was invited to the Washington, D.C., International, but Mrs. du Pont declined the invitation. She and Hanford didn't want to risk running him over soft going as a three-year-old, especially with his stifle problem. There would be plenty of other opportunities to take on the world.

Although Bald Eagle went on to win the

International wire to wire, he had to settle for just champion handicap honors, as Kelso ran away with the Horse of the Year title, only the second gelding to do so since year-end awards were officially designated in 1936. (The other was Calumet Farm's Armed in 1947.) Kelso was also named champion three-year-old male.

That Christmas, Hanford had special cards made up showing Kelso in his stall, peering down over the webbing. Sitting under the webbing, looking up, were Hanford's two dogs, Sketch and Mickey. The card read: "Merry Christmas and a Happy New Year 1960, from Kelso, Sketch, Mickey, and the Hanfords."

Just before Christmas, Kelso had shipped to Santa Anita to run in the seven-furlong Malibu Stakes but was scratched after wrenching his stifle. The inflammation persisted, and he was forced to miss the Maturity Stakes as well. So, Hanford sent him back to Mrs. du Pont's farm in January for some well-earned R&R. In nine starts in 1960, Kelso won eight, including six consecutive stakes at six different distances. He won two titles and equaled or broke three track records. It would have been difficult for anyone to believe at the time that this was merely the tip of the iceberg.

KELSO

CHAPTER 6

The Master's Swan Song

Following his brief stay at the farm, Kelso was sent to Aiken, South Carolina, to begin training for his four-year-old campaign. Many of the leading stables wintered in Aiken, including Greentree, Woody Stephens, and F. Ambrose Clark. Although the weather was cold on occasion, the deep, sandy track never froze and was excellent for getting horses fit and ready for their debuts. Training culminated in late March with the running of the Aiken Trials, where horses, including the two-year-olds, competed in sprints. Many a youngster would come up north afterward and win first time out at a good price, being the Aiken Trials were not listed in the *Daily Racing Form* past performances.

Kelso thrived at Aiken, and during his first winter there he grew about an inch to reach nearly sixteen hands. His girth thickened from seventy and a half inches to seventy-two inches, his neck filled out significantly, and though still not the most attractive of horses, he now strutted around with a sense of nobility.

One of the regulars at Aiken was New Jersey-based trainer Joe Kulina, whose eleven-year-old son, Bobby, would later visit with Kelso regularly and develop a deep affection for the horse. When Bobby first saw him in the winter of 1961, however, the horse was not what he had expected. "That's Kelso?" he said. Equine heroes were supposed to look like Black Beauty or Man o' War, especially to an eleven-year-old.

Bobby went on to become racing secretary at Monmouth Park and Meadowlands, and eventually vice president and general manager of Thoroughbred racing at Monmouth. Even after four decades, Kelso remains his all-time favorite horse.

When Kelso arrived in New York in the spring of 1961, a new person entered his life. During the winter Tommy Trotter had replaced Jimmy Kilroe as racing secretary for the New York Racing Association, and Kelso would make Trotter's first year on the job interesting to say the least.

From the time Tommy was a kid, he had known Carl

Hanford. Hanford worked for Tommy's father, trainer Tobe Trotter, on the New England circuit and often stayed with the family. Although he had remained close with Hanford through the years, Tommy now had the unenviable job of having to weight his Horse of the Year in some of the top handicaps in the country. If people thought Trotter was going to take it easy on his old friend's horse, they were grossly mistaken. Having worked for John B. Campbell and Kilroe, he knew he had a tradition to uphold. But no matter how much weight Trotter piled on Kelso's back, neither Hanford nor Mrs. du Pont ever complained.

That spring a new hero emerged whose rags-to-riches story captured the imagination of the country. His name was Carry Back, an obscurely bred son of Saggy who was bred and trained by a small-time, outspoken horseman named Jack Price and owned by Price's wife, Katherine. Price threw away the book in his training of Carry Back, running him an incredible twenty-one times as a two-year-old. Carry Back's first thirteen starts were at distances from three to five and a half furlongs, and his first start was on January 29, meaning the colt began racing just after turning two.

Despite this unorthodox and arduous campaign, Carry Back stormed through Florida in the winter of '61, winning the Everglades, Flamingo, and Florida Derby. After finishing second in the Wood Memorial, he came from the clouds to win the Kentucky Derby and Preakness with spectacular late charges. An injury suffered in the Belmont Stakes ended his fairy tale attempt to sweep the Triple Crown, as he plodded home in seventh behind 65-1 shot Sherluck.

Hanford, meanwhile, was going slowly with Kelso, pointing him for the Handicap Triple Crown. With the May 30 Metropolitan Handicap coming up fast, Hanford desperately needed a race for Kelso. Fortunately, Trotter wrote a seven-furlong allowance race as the feature on May 19, with Kelso carrying 124 pounds. Seven overmatched opponents showed up, and although Kelso could have won by the length of the stretch, Arcaro knew he couldn't win by too much with the weights for the Met Mile due out shortly. After cruising to the lead at the eighth pole, Arcaro grabbed a tight hold of Kelso and had to strangle him to keep the margin down to a length and a half.

After dismounting, the first person he saw was

Dickie Jenkins. "Dickie, you know what?" he said. "There's no telling how good this horse really is. This is a runnin' sonofabitch."

Kelso was now at the mercy of Trotter for the first time. Although Kelso had never carried more than 124 pounds in his career, Trotter made him the top weight at 130. In the 1950s four-year-olds Tom Fool, Native Dancer, High Gun, and Gallant Man all carried 130 in the Met, and Trotter felt Kelso fit in that class.

The Met was an important race, being the first leg of the Handicap Triple Crown. The Suburban and Brooklyn handicaps, both run at a mile and a quarter, comprised the other two legs. It took a combination of speed, toughness, and class to win going a flat mile against top horses. The winner then would have to come back a little over a month later, carrying higher weights, and win going ten furlongs twice in less than two weeks. Only two horses — Whisk Broom II in 1913 and Greentree's Tom Fool in 1953 — had managed to sweep all three races.

Kelso was sent off as the even-money favorite, with his main threat being the Gulfstream Park Handicap winner Tudor Way, who was in with 126 pounds, one more than Mail Order, winner of the Grey Lag Handicap. A crowd of 65,569 poured into The Big A, many eager to see the stakes return of the reigning Horse of the Year.

Cain Hoy Stable's All Hands, who had finished third in several top stakes that winter and spring, including the Grey Lag, had good early speed. Carrying thirteen pounds less than Kelso, All Hands and his rider Manny Ycaza, known for his aggressive riding style, took the offensive right from the start. The Cain Hoy colt disposed of Mail Order early and opened up a clear lead heading into the clubhouse turn, while running into a good headwind. Kelso, meanwhile, had only two horses beat and had seven lengths to make up. As the field hit the quarter pole, All Hands was still winging on the front and took a three-length lead into the stretch. Kelso still was back in seventh, and it looked as if it would take a miracle finish for him to overtake All Hands.

All Hands still led by three passing the eighth pole, as Arcaro desperately tried to find clear sailing through the field. He cut to the inside, but found his path blocked. Jenkins, standing at the rail, thought, "He's not gonna get nothin'." Arcaro had no other choice but to yank Kelso to the outside. By the time he finally was able to get a clear run to the wire, all looked hopeless. All Hands wasn't tiring, and Kelso had too much ground to make up. In the final sixteenth Kelso was relentless as he chopped into All Hands' lead with every stride. The wire was coming up fast. It was going to be close. Thousands in the grandstand simultaneously leaned to the right, trying to get Kelso home with body language. He gave one final thrust in the shadow of the wire and stuck his neck just in front at the finish. Kelso had closed his final quarter in a shade under :24 to complete the mile in 1:35 3/5.

A symphony of cheers awaited the champ as he returned to the winner's circle. Arcaro dismounted, and for the first time since he began riding Kelso, he described him as "great." Having ridden some of the greatest horses of all time, such as Citation and Whirlaway, that was a word Arcaro used very sparingly.

The next stop for Kelso was the Whitney Stakes. Normally run in August at Saratoga, the race was moved up to June at Belmont. Hanford decided to bring Kelso back eighteen days later for the nine-furlong race, knowing that under the allowance conditions the Horse of the Year would get to carry the same weight as he did in the Met.

All Hands came back for another crack at Kelso, but this time, instead of pulling thirteen pounds, he received twenty pounds. The hard-knocking Polylad also entered, under 112 pounds, as did the stakes-placed Our Hope, who was trained by Joe Kulina.

Kelso was the overwhelming favorite at 2-5. Unlike in the Met, All Hands folded early, as Kelso charged past him nearing the head of the stretch. The only threat came from Our Hope, who was in receipt of nineteen pounds from Kelso. As they straightened into the stretch, Our Hope, under Pete Anderson, pulled alongside Kelso.

Watching the race on TV were Bobby Kulina and his mother and sister. Bobby had not yet become infatuated with Kelso, and he cheered on his father's horse. The three of them had been at Dorney Park, an amusement park, that afternoon on a church outing, and they had stopped in a bar on the way home to see the telecast.

They watched as Our Hope held on doggedly and wouldn't let Kelso get by him. At the wire it was Our

Hope by a head. What they hadn't seen, however, was Our Hope leaning into Kelso and repeatedly pushing him in on the rail. They were so close, Anderson was unable to switch his whip to his left hand.

The jubilant Kulinas left the bar not knowing there was a steward's inquiry. It wasn't until Joe got home that they were told that after a long deliberation the stewards had disqualified Our Hope. Anderson said he felt he was just race riding and hadn't bothered Kelso enough to change the race's outcome. When the stewards asked him about the incident, he said, "I just did what Arcaro would do in the same situation."

Not only did the stewards disqualify Our Hope, they suspended Anderson. Whenever Anderson ran into Dickie Jenkins, he'd say, "You sonofabitches stole that race off me."

Mrs. du Pont felt it was unfortunate that Kelso had to win that way, and she felt bad for the Kulinas. Shortly after the race she sent a letter to the Kulinas, apologizing for the turn of events.

With the Whitney scare out of the way, Hanford turned his attention to the Suburban Handicap. His longtime friend Tommy Trotter could have raised Kelso a pound, or even two, after his two close finishes and no one would have batted an eye. But Trotter packed 133 pounds on the horse, who would be giving away as much as twenty-seven pounds. After Tom Fool had won the Met Mile, his weight was lowered to 128 pounds for the Suburban.

Lack of top quality competition had led Trotter to increase Kelso's weight by three pounds. King Ranch's Disperse had won the Hempstead Handicap, placed in the Excelsior Handicap, and was the 5-1 second choice as part of an entry with Whitley, who had won a couple of stakes two years earlier but had just two allowance victories to his credit this season. Disperse was in at 110 pounds; Whitley at 112. The stayer, Don Poggio, runner-up to Kelso in the 1960 Jockey Club Gold Cup, was next at 7-1 and was the second high weight at 123. At 121 was the 1960 Wood Memorial winner Francis S., who was at nearly 13-1. Nickel Boy, coming off a third to Polylad in the Massachusetts Handicap, was at 17-1 and carrying 112.

The temperature neared eighty degrees on this Fourth of July afternoon. Kelso, the 3-5 favorite, was never in any danger as he tracked the leaders in fourth.

He did have to steady briefly behind horses, but once Arcaro gave him breathing room, he burst to the lead turning for home, and then drew off with ease. Once again, Arcaro was trying to throttle him down in the final furlong to escape the itchy trigger finger of Mr. Trotter. But even with Arcaro applying a full nelson, Kelso still won by five lengths over Nickel Boy, while running his final quarter in :24 2/5.

When it came time for the weights for the Brooklyn Handicap, run eighteen days later, Trotter went to the record books and saw that Tom Fool had won under 136 pounds in 1953, as had Alfred Vanderbilt's Discovery as a five-year-old in 1936. Even though no other Brooklyn winner had ever carried that much weight, Trotter decided to pack Kelso down with 136 pounds, giving him the chance to emulate racing's last Handicap Triple Crown winner.

Hanford wouldn't complain about Trotter's weights, but Jenkins had had enough. He felt that three pounds was too much to raise the horse at this high level. He went to Trotter, whom he had gotten to know well, and said, "Hey, Tommy, why do you want to keep putting these kind of weights on this horse for?" But

Trotter stood firm and told him that's what he felt Kelso deserved.

So, here was Kelso, the one-time scrawny, ratty-looking horse, burdened with a hefty 136 pounds. There is an old racetrack saying: weight will stop a freight train. That's what many of the best handicap horses in the country were hoping as they lined up to take on Kelso, who was conceding from twelve to thirty pounds to his nine opponents.

Among those entered against Kelso were Calumet Farm's Yorky, winner of the Widener Handicap; Don Poggio and Our Hope, coming off a one-two finish in the Monmouth Handicap; Polylad, the MassCap winner; and Divine Comedy, who was coming off an overnight victory at Belmont and who would go on to win the Saratoga Handicap the following month.

But it wasn't the competition or the weight that was Kelso's main obstacle. It was the stifling one hundred-degree heat that descended on New York City. That would make the 136 pounds more likely to take a toll on the lightly built gelding.

On July 22, 35,013 perspiring fans gathered at The Big A to see history made. Arcaro knew this would be his last year riding, and he wanted nothing more than to go out in a blaze of glory by accomplishing one of the few major feats that had escaped him in his long and illustrious career. Hanford said nothing to him before the race. Arcaro had won nine races in a row aboard Kelso, and it was in historic, pressure-packed races like this that he shined.

But right from the start, Arcaro knew the Brooklyn was going to be nothing resembling a textbook race. Divine Comedy, breaking from post ten on the far outside, was gunned to the lead by Mickey Solomone, who opened up a huge advantage. Going into the clubhouse turn, he already was six in front. Francis S. tracked the leader, while Yorky held a slim advantage over Kelso for third. Down the backstretch, Divine Comedy, in receipt of eighteen pounds from Kelso, opened up by almost ten lengths after a testing half in :46 2/5. Arcaro never panicked. He didn't regard Divine Comedy as a serious threat and was more interested in controlling the pack of horses that were chasing him. He eased Kelso into third and was content to keep him some fifteen lengths off the lead.

But as they hit the half-mile pole and headed

around the far turn, Divine Comedy, who would prove at Saratoga he was a better horse than Arcaro thought, still led by eight lengths, with Kelso another four lengths behind longshot Francis S. Kelso had just run his third quarter in an exacting :23 flat and still was a dozen lengths out of it. Tommy Trotter, watching from the clubhouse, started getting a bad feeling. Maybe he had blown it. "He has no chance," he thought. "There's no way he's ever going to catch that horse. I think I made a mistake."

Arcaro began nudging Kelso along to get him to start closing the gap. At the quarter pole Divine Comedy's lead was down to three lengths, as Kelso ranged up behind Francis S. Down the stretch Divine Comedy still had something left. Arcaro smacked Kelso a couple of times with the whip, and he kept coming, cutting into the lead with workmanlike precision. Passing the eighth pole, Divine Comedy was desperately holding on to a length lead, with Kelso now lapped on Francis S.

But the heat and the weight were getting to Kelso, so Arcaro went to the whip again inside the eighth pole. Kelso dug in and gave another surge that carried him right on by Divine Comedy inside the sixteenth pole. The grandstand was rocking, as Kelso drew off on his way into the history books. He crossed the wire a length and a quarter in front of Divine Comedy. Despite the heat and weight, he had closed his final quarter in :24 2/5 to complete the mile and a quarter in 2:01 3/5, two-fifths of a second off Sword Dancer's track record.

A rousing ovation from the appreciative crowd awaited Kelso as he returned to the winner's circle. Not only had he swept the Handicap Triple Crown, he had extended his winning streak to eleven races.

Hanford gave Kelso a few weeks to get over the Brooklyn and then began gearing him up for the one-mile Washington Park Handicap at Arlington. He sent Dickie Jenkins and Billy Hall with the horse, as he had done the year before. Shortly after arriving, Kelso was scheduled to be shod, so Jenkins and Hall waited for the blacksmith to arrive. Shoeing Kelso was not an ordinary procedure, as the horse had very tender feet and thin hoof walls. To pass the time, Jenkins went into the tack room and took a nap. When he awoke, he opened the screen door and saw a large pile of hoof clippings on the floor of the shed row.

He feared the worst. "Hey, Bill, is that from Kelso's foot?" he asked Hall, not really wanting to hear the answer.

"Yeah," Hall answered.

"Jesus Christ, this sonofabitch ain't gonna be able to walk in the morning," he said. Jenkins thought Hall would wake him up, or at least would know what to tell the blacksmith about the horse's tender feet. But in the end he took the blame for sleeping while Kelso was being shod.

Sure enough, the following morning, Kelso came out of his stall as if he were "walking on eggs." Stepping onto the gravel path, Kelso began lifting his foot quickly off the ground. When Hanford arrived, he saw the way Kelso was walking, and after finding out what had happened, he chewed Jenkins out for falling asleep.

A quarter-inch thick sealer was put on the foot, which seemed to help, except when Kelso walked on the gravel path. To make matters worse, the track, even though officially listed as good, was packed down rock hard for the Washington Park Handicap, and it stung Kelso's foot every time he came down on it. Carrying

132 pounds, he dropped back to tenth and was boxed in for a good part of the race, eventually finishing a non-threatening fourth behind Carter Handicap winner Chief of Chiefs. Finishing second was Talent Show, whom Kelso had easily defeated in the Suburban.

After the race, as Jenkins was unsaddling Kelso, Arcaro told him, "Jesus, Dickie, this sonofabitch couldn't handle that track at all. He kept changing leads on me."

September meant weight-for-age races, and that meant Tommy Trotter now was just another guy in a suit. Kelso was out of his clutches, at least until the following year. The Woodward, run at the end of the month, introduced a new foe for Kelso. Carry Back had returned from his Belmont injury, winning an allowance race at Atlantic City and then the Jerome Handicap under 128 pounds. He was no threat in the United Nations Handicap, his first attempt on the grass.

Divine Comedy was back for another attempt at thievery, with Whodunit and Tompion completing the small field. Kelso, under 126 pounds, was 1-2, with Carry Back, at 120 on the scale, next at 4-1. Bill Shoemaker was on Divine Comedy this time, and he tried the same tactics as Mickey Solomone. But despite carving out a sharp pace of :46 1/5 and 1:10 flat, he could never shake free from Kelso, who this time was more inclined to stalk his prey.

At the quarter pole, Kelso was all over him, as Carry Back futilely attempted to close in from last. They had blazed the mile in 1:34 4/5, which equaled Count Fleet's track record. That meant nothing to Kelso. Once they straightened into the stretch, the champ merely stretched his muscles and bounded clear. Without Trotter's watchful eye glaring at him from the grandstand, Arcaro let Kelso roll, and the gelding coasted home by eight lengths. Carry Back tried to rally but fell a half-length short of catching Divine Comedy for second. Although Kelso had won eased up, his time of 2:00 equaled Whisk Broom II's forty-eight-year-old track record. That record wouldn't be broken until Forego ran a fifth of a second faster fourteen years later.

The Jockey Club Gold Cup three weeks later proved nothing more than a workout, as Kelso merely toyed with his three overmatched opponents, winning by five lengths in a virtual gallop.

It was time for his grass debut in the Washington, D.C., International on November 11. The foreign invaders didn't look exceptionally strong, and it appeared as if Kelso's main threat would come from fellow American T. V. Lark, who had won the Hawthorne Gold Cup and Knickerbocker, Los Angeles, and Santa Catalina handicaps that year.

The week before the International, Kelso had appeared on the cover of *Sports Illustrated* magazine, with the caption, "America's Kelso Against Them All."

The gelding had never been on the turf and had never run in a race where they used a tape start instead of a gate, so Hanford schooled him at Laurel Park, teaching him to break into a run without a starting gate. As the tape was lifted, an assistant starter waved his arms at Kelso while Hanford, standing on the other side, clapped his hands loudly.

Walking from the barn to the track before the race, Hanford was directly behind the Irish filly, Sail Cheoil, who began lashing out with her back legs any time another horse got close to her. When Hanford saw Arcaro in the paddock, he told him, "Watch out for this filly. She kicks like heck."

Kelso handled the tape start like the pro he was, and Arcaro put him right on the lead, with Johnny

Longden and T. V. Lark lapped on him. After a half-mile the pair pulled clear of the pack. Arcaro didn't like his position and knew he had been outfoxed by Longden. T. V. Lark was an experienced grass horse who was breathing down Kelso's neck every step of the way. By the quarter-pole, they had opened ten lengths on the field and still were locked together. Kelso battled hard, but T. V. Lark stuck his head in front at the eighth pole. Kelso wasn't through and kept fighting back. But at the wire, it was T. V. Lark by three-quarters of a length, and the time of 2:26 1/5 for the mile and a half established a new course record.

After the race Arcaro was furious at himself. "I guarantee you if they'd run this race tomorrow, we'd win," he said. "I'd know what to do this time. This horse never should have gotten beat."

The following morning Hanford noticed that Kelso's hind hock had swelled up to "the size of a football." He had no idea how it happened. A short time later, state veterinarian David Pace showed up and asked Hanford, "How's your horse's leg?"

"How did you know about that?" Hanford asked him.

"I saw it happen," he said. "That Irish filly kicked him right smack in the hock over at the start. It sounded like a cannon went off."

Not only had Kelso's hock swelled, but he also came out of the race with sprains in his front and hind legs. He was sent down to Aiken to recuperate and get ready for the 1962 season. He received year-end honors for champion older horse and his second Horse of the Year award. His rival T. V. Lark was named champion grass horse.

That winter Kelso lost his groom and his jockey. Bill Hall quit, and Arcaro retired after thirty-one years in the saddle. He had won 4,779 races, second only to Johnny Longden, and earned a record $30,039,543.

In the spring of 1997, Arcaro was in Texas being honored by Lone Star Park. It was to be his final public appearance. At dinner he and Chick Lang, former executive vice-president and general manager at Pimlico, were discussing old times.

"Eddie," Lang said, "the stock question everyone always asks you is, who's the best horse you've ever ridden? And you've always answered Citation."

It was then that Arcaro jumped in: "Chick, I'm

going to tell you something I've never told anybody, and I promised myself I would never say it unless I outlived Jimmy Jones (Citation's trainer). I'd never say this in public while Jimmy is still alive, because if I did, he'd be on the phone the next day and he'd really be upset with me. But between you and me, I'm going to tell you right here and now that the greatest horse I ever rode, without question, was Kelso. He could do anything. He could sprint, go two miles, run on off tracks, fast tracks, inside, outside — anything!"

Arcaro didn't outlive Jones and never made his feelings public. He died in November of 1997, four years before Jones. But his words are still crystal clear in Lang's head. After all, when "The Master" says for the first time after thirty-six years that Kelso is the greatest horse he ever rode, it's something not easily forgotten.

CHAPTER 7

The Purple Gang

K elso went into the 1962 season with back-to-back Horse of the Year titles, becoming the first horse to accomplish that feat since Whirlaway in 1941 and '42. But Kelso was just getting warmed up.

Now five years old, he spent another tranquil winter in Aiken, enjoying his afternoons of grazing and getting to know his new groom, Lawrence Joseph Thomas Fitzpatrick, better known as "Fitz." Kelso was able to spend some down time outside his stall for the first time in his career, and he loved every minute of it. Fitz had worked for Hanford for years, and when Billy Hall quit, Hanford gave him Kelso to rub. Fitz only referred to the horse as "Kelly," after the favorite color of every Irishman — Kelly green.

As Kelso lived a contented life of leisure in South Carolina, the rest of the country was caught up in

Derby fever. In 1962 the two names on everyone's lips in Florida were Ridan and Sir Gaylord, and it came as a crushing blow when Sir Gaylord dropped out with an eleventh-hour injury after rattling off four straight victories, including the Bahamas and Everglades stakes. Ridan, trained by LeRoy Jolley, won the Florida Derby and Blue Grass Stakes and brought a record of ten victories in thirteen starts into the Kentucky Derby. Sent off at even-money in the Derby, he could manage only a third behind the 8-1 Decidedly. Local Maryland horse Greek Money then upset Ridan by a nose in the Preakness after a controversial stretch run, in which Ridan's rider, Manny Ycaza, reached over and locked arms with John Rotz, on Greek Money, after attempting to elbow him in the chest.

With Kelso back in New York after his winter vacation, Carl Hanford decided to follow the previous year's game plan and use an allowance race as the champ's prep for the Metropolitan Handicap. With the retirement of Eddie Arcaro, Hanford gave the mount on Kelso to Bill Shoemaker. It wasn't exactly the marriage Hanford was hoping for.

As the Met Mile drew closer, Hanford realized he

was not going to get the prep race he wanted for Kelso. Tommy Trotter did his part by writing several allowance races for the horse, but word was out that the trainer was on the lookout for a prep, and none of the races filled. So Hanford had to send Kelso into battle off a six and a half-month layoff without a prep. To make matters worse, Kelso was assigned an outrageous 133 pounds, conceding ten pounds to Carry Back, and from thirteen to twenty-five pounds to the rest of the field. This was an unusually heavy burden for a horse making his first start of the year. Still, the crowd sent him off at 3-5.

In a rare occurrence, Kelso simply never fired. He raced evenly the whole way, finishing a non-threatening sixth, as Carry Back drew off to a two and a half-length score in a track record-equaling 1:33 3/5. It was a disheartening introduction for Shoemaker, who said simply, "He just didn't have it. The 133 and not having had a race this year made the difference."

The next stop for Kelso was the Nassau County Stakes at Belmont, or so everyone thought. With the horse coming off one of the worst races of his career, Hanford wanted to give him an easy spot. Even though the Nassau County was basically a prep for the Suburban Handicap and didn't normally draw the best horses, Hanford didn't want Kelso to have to give away a ton of weight. He knew a victory would have his buddy Trotter piling on the weight again for the Suburban.

Hanford noticed that Trotter had written a one-mile allowance race on the same day as the Nassau County for which Kelso was eligible, not having won a race since the previous October. Hanford didn't say a word. On entry day he calmly walked into the racing office and dropped Kelso's name in the entry box for the allowance race. He told the entry clerk if the race didn't fill, he'd enter Kelso in the Nassau County. The entry clerk raced into Trotter's office to tell him the news.

"Tommy, Kelso is going in the allowance instead of the stakes," he said to a surprised Trotter. "He told me to tell you if the race doesn't fill he'll go in the Nassau County."

With all the trainers caught by surprise, a field of six was entered. Kelso was coming off an uncharacteristic dull effort, and they thought perhaps they had a shot to knock off the champ. The race went with all six horses, including the quick-footed Rose Net, who later that year would set a new track record of 1:21 1/5 for seven furlongs at Aqueduct. Kelso, in light with 117 pounds, had little trouble, as he flew home his last quarter in :23 3/5 to beat the hard-knocking Garwol by two and a quarter lengths in 1:35 3/5. It was a perfect prep for the Suburban, run eighteen days later.

But the Suburban would not unfold as the easy romp the Kelso camp anticipated. Allen Jerkens saw to that. In 1975 Jerkens, at age forty-five, became the youngest trainer at that time to be inducted into the National Museum of Racing Hall of Fame. His ascent up racing's highest peak began on July 4, 1962. That date also marked the birth of the nickname "The Giant Killer," the moniker Jerkens carried the next four decades after upsetting some of racing's biggest stars.

A little over a month earlier, Jerkens had taken a job as trainer for Jack Dreyfus, who had recently purchased a farm in Ocala, Florida, naming it Hobeau Farm, because of his "tendency to be a bum." Dreyfus was hardly a bum although he often dressed like one. He was president of a $300 million mutual investment firm that bore his name. The Dreyfus Fund lion, strolling through the streets and out of the subways of New York City, appeared in the company's television commercials and became a familiar figure on television sets all across America.

Dreyfus had six horses in training at the time, and Jerkens agreed to become the stable's private trainer once it was fully stocked. One morning at breakfast, when Dreyfus and his farm manager, Elmer Heubeck, were seducing Jerkens for the job, Dreyfus told Jerkens about his new farm and his stallion, Beau Gar, and added that he felt one of Beau Gar's sons, Beau Purple, had potential.

Jerkens did not share Dreyfus' enthusiasm for Beau Purple, and, in fact, liked several of the fillies much more. Although the colt had speed and natural talent, he also had a common streak. He was a frontrunner who disliked competition. Jerkens knew if he didn't drill him hard and try to toughen him, he would continue to quit whenever another horse looked him in the eye.

Not only did Jerkens consider Beau Purple a second-rate horse, but the colt no longer qualified for allowance races, which meant he had no other place to go but stakes company.

"What are you going to do with him?" Dreyfus asked Jerkens.

"I don't know," Jerkens answered. "He's out of conditions, so I have to find something for him."

"Well, don't be afraid to nominate him to stakes," Dreyfus said.

Entries for the Suburban Handicap happened to be closing that same day. At 10:30 at night, Jerkens called Trotter. He told him he hated to bother him at home, but he wanted to nominate Beau Purple to the Suburban. There were only eleven nominations, so Trotter was thrilled by the addition.

Beau Purple had showed signs of brilliance, racing for trainer Maje Odom, but only when left unchallenged. He romped in the Appleton Handicap at Gulfstream and easily won two allowance races in New York, including a track record-equaling victory in 1:33 3/5 for the mile. In his last start for Odom, he was challenged for the lead and stopped to a walk, getting beat seventeen lengths; hardly credentials to compete against the mighty Kelso and Carry Back going a mile

The mighty Kelso ruled horse racing in the 1960s, reigning as Horse of the Year for an unprecedented five years.

Kelso received courage in good measure from his sire, Your Host (above), who survived a severe leg fracture. Your Host was by Alibhai (top), a son of the great English sire Hyperion. Maid of Flight (right), Kelso's dam, was a sturdy, useful runner by 1943 Triple Crown winner Count Fleet (below).

Kelso was raised at Allaire du Pont's Woodstock Farm (below) in Maryland. Over the course of his long career, Kelso, along with Mrs. du Pont (above, with daughter Lana, and left, leading her star in), became a familiar sight in the winner's circle, especially at Aqueduct and Belmont Park.

In addition to Mrs. du Pont, Kelso's devoted human companions
included exercise rider Dick Jenkins (top) and trainer Carl Hanford
(above left). Kelso also had a number of canine friends over the years
(above right, with the human crew).

John Block (above), a contract rider for Mrs. du Pont, was the first of many jockeys to ride Kelso. But the two jockeys most closely identified with the great gelding are Ismael "Milo" Valenzuela (right) and Eddie Arcaro (below).

In the fall of his three-year-old season, Kelso reeled off six straight stakes victories, including the Jerome (above, Kelso on outside), the Lawrence Realization (top), and the Jockey Club Gold Cup (below), a race with which he would become synonymous. Kelso earned his first Horse of the Year title that year.

At four Kelso continued to power his
way to victory with Arcaro aboard. He
added the New York Handicap Triple
Crown to his resume, winning the
Metropolitan, Suburban (right), and
Brooklyn (top left) handicaps during
the summer. That fall he added
the Woodward (above) and
another Jockey Club Gold Cup
(top right).

In 1962 at five, Kelso added victories in the Stymie (below), Governor's Plate (above), Woodward, and, of course, the Jockey Club Gold Cup. At six, instead of wintering as usual in Aiken, S.C., Kelso began his season in Florida, winning the Seminole and Gulfstream Park handicaps. He added the John B. Campbell Handicap at Bowie in Maryland (above left) before getting a vacation. Kelso returned in June with a victory in the Nassau County at Aqueduct (top).

Kelso rolled through the summer of 1963 with victories in the Suburban (bottom), Whitney (below right), Aqueduct, and Woodward (top). Winning the Woodward with "speed to spare," Kelso was joined in the winner's circle by (inset, left to right) Dick Jenkins; Carl Hanford; Mrs. du Pont's father, Samuel A. Crozer; Lana du Pont, and Mrs. du Pont. Kelso ended the season with his fourth victory in the Jockey Club Gold Cup and his fourth Horse of the Year title.

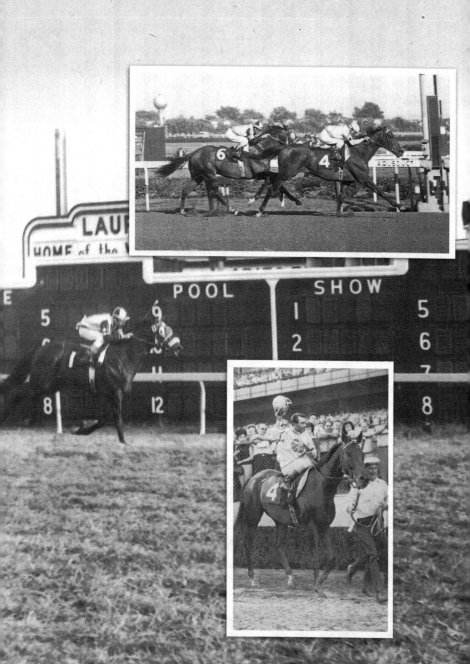

In 1964 as a seven-year-old, Kelso had a major nemesis to contend with in Gun Bow, but Kelso prevailed in the Aqueduct (opposite, top). The gelding went on to add his fifth Jockey Club Gold Cup (opposite, bottom), and he finally captured the elusive Washington, D.C., International (center and right), defeating Gun Bow again and setting a course record in the process. Before the race Kelso and Dick Jenkins met the jockey and trainer of the Russian horse Aniline (top), who finished third.

In the twilight of his career, Kelso still proved he could win with style, taking the Diamond State Stakes (above) and the Stymie (left) easily. And he had plenty of strength and heart left to grit out a nose victory over Malicious in a hard-fought Whitney (below, Kelso on outside).

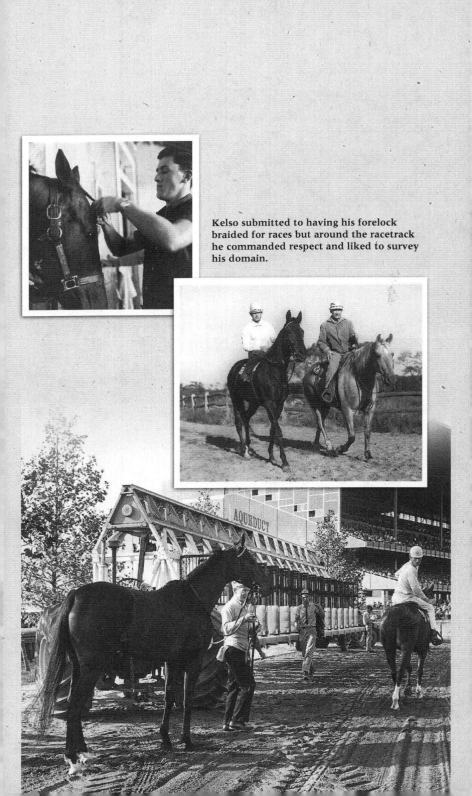

Kelso submitted to having his forelock braided for races but around the racetrack he commanded respect and liked to survey his domain.

Upon retirement, Kelso began a new career, that of show jumper. He learned his new trade from Alison Cram (right), a former junior dressage champion. Kelso demonstrated his new ability at Saratoga (above). Mrs. du Pont also rode her great champion around Woodstock (below).

In October 1983, after enjoying seventeen years of retirement, Kelso (right and above left) joined two other grand geldings, John Henry (above middle) and Forego (above right), at Belmont Park for Jockey Club Gold Cup festivities. Kelso (top) and Forego, then fourteen, were paraded for fans, while John Henry, at age eight, was competing in the race. Kelso would suffer a fatal bout of colic the next day.

Kelso was buried at Woodstock, where he once galloped and where his spirit gallops still.

and a quarter.

Jerkens began "fiddling around" with Beau Purple, breezing him six furlongs in 1:19, galloping out a mile in 1:45 and a mile and a quarter in 2:09. Jerkens knew he had to really let him roll if he was going to have him ready to compete against Kelso. He put his best exercise rider, George Wallace, up, and Beau Purple worked six furlongs in a blazing 1:10. Now, Jerkens needed to take some of the speed away, so two days before the Suburban, he sent him out for a slow mile breeze. But Beau Purple was feeling too good, and he wound up working in 1:37, galloping out a mile and one-eighth in 1:50...two days before he had to run a mile and a quarter.

Jerkens thought, "If this sonofagun isn't bothered at all by this work, he's gonna put in the race of his life." When Jerkens went to the barn in the afternoon, Beau Purple was chowing down his dinner. That was the final sign the trainer was looking for.

Jerkens' confidence began to rub off on jockey Bill Boland. The following day Dickie Jenkins was in the racing office and overheard Boland saying, "They better not let me get out there by five at the three-eighths pole, 'cause I'll give this sucker a breather, and they're gonna have to run to catch his ass with 115 pounds on him."

Only four horses showed up for the Suburban. Kelso was carrying 132 pounds, six more than Carry Back, seventeen more than Beau Purple, and twenty-three more than Garwol, who would pop up in just about every big race hoping to pick up a piece of the pot.

Just as Boland had said, Beau Purple shot to the front and quickly opened up by three lengths. Shoemaker had Kelso in third, six lengths behind. Boland was able to slow the pace down with a quarter in :24 3/5 and a half in :48 4/5. Shoemaker was busy watching John Rotz on Carry Back, just behind him, and paid little attention to Beau Purple. When the field hit the three-quarters in a sluggish 1:12 4/5, and Beau Purple was still alone on the front end, it became obvious that Kelso was ripe for another upset.

Shoemaker set Kelso down for his drive, but Beau Purple was motoring. He went his next quarter in :23 4/5 and his final quarter in :24 flat. No one, not even Kelso, was going to cut into those kinds of fractions, especially carrying seventeen more pounds. Beau

Purple beat Kelso by two and a half lengths, with Carry Back struggling home in fourth. Beau Purple's time of 2:00 3/5 established an Aqueduct record. This would not be the last Kelso saw of the Hobeau horse.

The big three showed up again ten days later for the mile and a quarter Monmouth Handicap. It would be Shoemaker's last ride aboard Kelso. Off his two stakes defeats Kelso's impost was lowered to 130 pounds, with Carry Back at 124 and Beau Purple at 117. A crowd of almost 33,000 packed Monmouth Park on a humid, overcast afternoon. When Ogden Phipps' Hitting Away charged to the lead at the start, Boland grabbed hold of Beau Purple and attempted to rate him. But the Hobeau horse was not fond of strangulation, and he fought Boland through quick fractions of :46 and 1:10. Kelso was in excellent position back in fourth, with Carry Back, under John Rotz, a couple of lengths behind him.

Leaving the half-mile pole, Boland had to let Beau Purple go and they pounced on Hitting Away. Instead of sending Kelso at that point, Shoemaker let Rotz and Carry Back steamroll past him on the outside. By the time Shoemaker did ask Kelso for his run, he had nowhere to go except to the inside, and the Shoe found himself trapped by Carry Back in a neatly wrapped box. Beau Purple took a brief lead but was spent fighting Boland and quickly gave way to Carry Back, who had clear sailing. Kelso finally found room along the inside, but it was too late to catch Carry Back, who hit the wire three lengths in front. Carry Back's time of 2:00 2/5 for the mile and a quarter established a track record.

So the mighty Kelso had now lost four of his last five starts, and some thought his two-year reign perhaps was over. For Jenkins the losses seemed to be a matter of Kelso's ability not being used to his best advantage. He didn't agree with Hanford's race strategy and thought Kelso should be allowed to use his speed and run freely. But Hanford didn't want to put the gelding in the battle that early carrying so much weight. Jenkins always spoke his mind and offered his opinions strongly and frequently. Hanford was the trainer, and for the most part wasn't interested in Jenkins' opinions, which created friction between them.

Hanford gave Kelso only two allowances races on the grass the rest of the summer, in order to have him fresh for the fall, historically a time during which the gelding always did his best running. Sharing Hanford's barn was Bert Mulholland, who had the George D. Widener horses, including the new leader of the three-year-old division, Jaipur. This fiery son of Nasrullah had rattled off victories in the Gotham, Withers, Jersey Derby, Belmont Stakes, and Choice Stakes, with his only defeat at three coming in the Preakness. In the historic Travers Stakes at Saratoga, Jaipur and Ridan engaged in one of the greatest duels the sport has ever seen when they raced eyeball to eyeball every step of the mile and a quarter. At the end it was the tenacious Jaipur who had his nose in front at the wire.

The main problem with Jaipur was that no one could handle him enough to get him to the racetrack, and it was Dickie Jenkins whom Mulholland sought to tame his wild beast. Everyone knew Jenkins' reputation for being able to handle the most ornery of horses. Even Jack Price approached him one day to work Carry Back, but Hanford wouldn't let him assist the enemy. So when Mulholland asked Jenkins to work with Jaipur, they had to wait for Hanford to leave. Then, Jenkins would take Jaipur to the opposite side of the barn, where no horses were stabled, and went about calming this "mean-ass horse." When he finished showing him who was the boss, he and Jaipur headed to the track with no problem.

Jenkins knew that Jaipur and Kelso would lock horns one day, but he relished the respect he was given and the challenges with which trainers presented him, and he would never refuse, regardless of who the horse was.

Following the Monmouth Handicap, Shoemaker decided to remain in California rather than travel east to ride Kelso, on whom he had had little success. Shoemaker was more of a finesse rider, and the often hardheaded Kelso needed an aggressive jockey who wasn't afraid to go to the whip. Hanford chose to replace Shoemaker with Ismael "Milo" Valenzuela, who came from a family of twenty-three children, two of whom were adopted. His older brother, Angel, who was a father figure to Milo, also was a jockey, riding the top-class Prince John for Max Gluck's Elmendorf Farm. Three other brothers — Mario, Alvino, and Santiago — also became jockeys, while another brother, Martin, trained horses for a while.

Valenzuela was born in McNary, Texas, in 1934. His father was a rancher from Porvenir, Mexico. His mother died at age fifty-one after suffering from pneumonia, and his father died three years later from an infection caused by a gunshot wound. Milo Valenzuela was put on his first horse at age three. By age eight, he and Angel were riding in match races. Milo got his start in the United States two years later, riding Quarter Horses. He won his debut at Rillito Downs in Tucson, Arizona, and before long he turned his attention to Thoroughbreds. He soon caught the eye of trainer Eddie Presnell who brought him to California as an apprentice. There, Milo flourished, and his first big win came aboard Porterhouse when they upset Swaps in the 1956 Californian. He also rode Nashville to victory over Bold Ruler and rode Mister Gus to win over Nashua. In 1958 Valenzuela teamed with famed Calumet Farm trainer Jimmy Jones to win the Kentucky Derby and Preakness with Tim Tam.

When Milo Valenzuela asked Arcaro for advice on riding Kelso, the Master told him, "Just remember, he doesn't want to be rushed. The stronger hold you take on the reins the more he'll give you when you ask him."

Arcaro also confided something else to Valenzuela. He told him that his only regret was that he and Kelso didn't retire together. He was afraid that the horse would be raced until he lost his luster and, in turn, his air of greatness.

Valenzuela and Kelso had immediate success, winning an allowance race on the grass at Saratoga and the Stymie Handicap at Aqueduct on September 19, in which Kelso conceded from fourteen to twenty-two pounds to his opponents. In between, he finished fourth in an allowance race on the grass at Atlantic City with Don Pierce aboard, in which he battled head and head on the lead early. Valenzuela's agent had booked him to ride elsewhere that day. But with just those two starts, Valenzuela could see immediately what Arcaro had described. Kelso wanted the rider to hold him together. Valenzuela didn't dare turn the horse's head loose, even when he was under a drive, or he would lose his action.

The next stop for Kelso was a showdown with Jaipur in the Woodward Stakes, only ten days after the Stymie. Had Dickie Jenkins done too good a job with the Widener colt? Jenkins wasn't worried. He never once thought Jaipur could beat Kelso. But Jaipur wasn't Kelso's only threat. Two of the gelding's conquerors — Beau Purple and T. V. Lark — also were entered. Under the weight-for-age conditions, Kelso and the other older horses carried 126 pounds, with the three-year-old Jaipur in with 120.

Kelso's spotty season hadn't affected his popularity, as more than 50,000 fans showed up at Aqueduct and made the champ the 4-5 favorite over Jaipur, who was second choice at 2-1. Beau Purple once again attempted to blow the field away, opening up by six lengths around the first turn and down the backstretch. The fractions were moderate over the deep track that was labeled good. Valenzuela was content to sit a couple of lengths behind Jaipur in third. When he asked Kelso to go nearing the half-mile pole, the result was swift and deadly. Kelso left Jaipur and blew by Beau Purple in a flash, opening a three-length lead at the quarter pole. Valenzuela sat motionless as Kelso cruised to a four and a half-length victory over Jaipur.

With two Jockey Club Gold Cups already to his credit, Kelso was bet down to 1-5 in the two-mile marathon a month later. The race was nothing more than a stroll around the Belmont oval, as Kelso coasted to a ten-length victory with his ears straight up, and his time of 3:19 4/5 broke the track record by three-fifths of a second.

Up to that point Hanford and Mrs. du Pont had remained immune to criticism, having done everything right with their horse. They planned the races well, never ducked anyone, and never complained about weight. That's what made their decision to run Kelso right back a week after the Gold Cup in the mile and a half Man o' War Stakes on the grass so puzzling. For the first time the media were critical of Mrs. du Pont, who had shown time and again that her affection for Kelso superseded all else. It was for that reason that the press couldn't understand why she would subject her beloved hero to a two-mile race and a mile and a half race in one week.

The Man o' War drew a twelve-horse field, including Kelso's shadow, Beau Purple, who was ripe off a victory in the Hawthorne Gold Cup just the week before. Some thought Jerkens was pushing his luck trying Kelso again under weight-for-age conditions.

When trainer Walter Kelley heard that Beau Purple

was running, he told Jerkens, "Don't tell me you're gonna take that horse over there and ask him to run against Kelso at even weights on the grass. I thought you were smarter than that."

Jerkens had had no intention of running Beau Purple, but when the horse came back from Chicago and was doing so well, he decided to take a chance. The race drew a top-class field that also included leading grass horses The Axe II, T. V. Lark, Wise Ship, and Harmonizing, along with Carry Back, fresh off a tenth-place finish in France's prestigious Prix de l'Arc de Triomphe, in which he was beaten only five and three-quarters lengths. There was great international flavor with the appearance of the French Derby winner Val de Loir.

Hanford has always taken the blame for getting Kelso beat in the Man o' War. He felt the Suburban was a fluke and still had no fear of Beau Purple. In the paddock Hanford told Valenzuela, "The horse to beat is The Axe. Beau Purple will go to the front, but you don't have to worry about him. He can't handle a mile and a half. Just wait until you get to the three-eighths, then move on him."

Beau Purple, as always, shot to the lead and skipped over the soft turf, maintaining a length and a half lead. Wise Ship and Kelso were in good striking range, but Valenzuela bided his time, as per instructions. By the time they hit the half-mile pole, Valenzuela was starting to get nervous. Beau Purple was still bounding along and showing no signs of coming back. "I better get going," Valenzuela thought. "That horse is too far in front." But by now, Beau Purple had strung out the field and was too strong to catch. He crossed the finish line two lengths in front of Kelso, who was six and a half lengths ahead of The Axe II. It was the Suburban all over again.

Things would be different in the Washington, D.C., International. This time, there was no way Beau Purple was going to steal another race on Kelso. The only other horse he had to worry about was Carry Back, who had just been beaten a nose by Mongo in the Trenton Handicap at Garden State Park. France was sending the King George VI and Queen Elizabeth Stakes and Grand Prix de Saint-Cloud winner Match II, who certainly had the talent and class to pose a serious threat. All Hanford told Valenzuela in the paddock was

to keep Beau Purple busy.

The 1962 International was to be Kelso's most frustrating defeat, as well as one of the best races he ever ran. The fans, having also been burned twice by ignoring Beau Purple, made the Hobeau colt the slight favorite at 2-1. It was the first time in twenty-three straight races that Kelso was not the favorite. When Beau Purple went to the lead, Valenzuela sent Kelso right up to hook him. They raced eyeball to eyeball for seven-eighths of a mile. This was not the way Beau Purple liked to run, and he suddenly gave up the fight and began his retreat to the back of the pack. Valenzuela now found himself alone on the lead and wasn't feeling good about his situation. He knew he had hit the front too soon. Kelso had battled hard to get there and was vulnerable to the fresh closers launching their bids behind him.

Around the far turn Carry Back came charging and pulled on even terms. Kelso dug in for another fight and wouldn't let Carry Back get past him. The pair dueled to the eighth pole as the crowd went wild. Just as Kelso put Carry Back away, however, a fresh Match II came flying at the leader. Kelso tried to battle back for a third time, but Match II was too strong and too fresh, and he wrested command with seventy yards to go, drawing clear to win by a length and a half. Kelso had four and a half lengths on Carry Back in third. In Kelso's entire career, Match II was the only horse ever to pass him in the stretch. Although he lost, Kelso ran his heart out, beating two of the best handicap horses in the country at their own game.

After the race Valenzuela was disconsolate over the loss. He ran into the jockey's room, buried his face in his hands, and sobbed for an hour before taking off his silks. Even with all his great victories aboard Kelso, Valenzuela would always say that this was the horse's greatest performance.

Hanford wanted Kelso to close out the year a winner, so he sent him to Garden State Park for the mile and a half Governor's Plate on the dirt, which Kelso won easily by five lengths, setting a track record and putting himself over the coveted million-dollar mark in earnings, joining Citation, Round Table, Nashua, and Carry Back.

Although 1962 was not one of Kelso's best years record-wise, he did turn in a number of unforgettable performances and nailed down his third consecutive Horse of the Year title, the first horse ever to achieve that honor.

Kelsoland

I nstead of heading down to Aiken until early spring, as he had done previously, Kelso was sent to Mrs. du Pont's farm for several weeks of R&R during the winter of 1962–63.

At Woodstock Farm, "Kelly" or "Kel," as he affectionately was known, lived in a huge stall with his name on the welcome mat. He had his own private mailbox to accommodate his volume of fan mail, which at one time reached five hundred letters a week, including one faithful fan who wrote to Kelso and Mrs. du Pont regularly from behind the Iron Curtain.

Kelso slept on a bed of sugar cane fibers, had a special embroidered blanket to keep him warm, and, because of recurring bouts with colic, he drank only bottled Mountain Valley spring water from Arkansas, costing five dollars a gallon. His insatiable sweet tooth was often pacified with ice cream sundaes, fresh carrots, or lumps of sugar that were individually wrapped in special paper bearing his name and picture, a gift from his fans.

His "family" over the years consisted of his longtime friends and stable ponies Spray and Pete, a stocky yellow cat who all but moved in with him, and an assorted group of canines who went by the names Rabbit, Cracker, Cookie, Sketch, Mickey, and his personal bodyguard, Charlie Potatoes, a little mutt who slept with Kelso every night and who rarely was out of his sight. Charlie was often seen at night stretched out across Kelso's head. These were just some of Kelso's many four-legged companions over the years.

Every afternoon Mrs. du Pont would get Kelso's mail from the large mailbox, on which was inscribed his name and address. One letter in particular, written on plain yellow paper by a youngster named John Price of Wilmington, Delaware, read: "Dear Kelso, God put us here at the same time, you to be a great race horse, and me to be a good boy for my mother and father..."

Maria Horodyska of Warsaw, Poland, wrote to Mrs. du Pont: "Shortly before the war we settled in Warsaw and went through the horrors of the German occupation and the tragedy of the resurrection of Warsaw. Our life was spared, but our health was very poor. In recent years, my husband has been working at the American Embassy and it was from the magazines and newspapers we get from there that we were able to keep up with Kelso. I thought it might give you pleasure to know that Kelso is loved and admired in faraway Poland."

Another letter from the mayor of Holland, Michigan, asked whether Kelso was available to be ridden by Prince Bernhard of the Netherlands during a ceremony in which the prince was dedicating the town's famed Dutch windmill that had been imported from that country.

A Peace Corps group about to leave for Thailand requested literature on Kelso so they could teach the Thai people all about the horse.

But of all of Kelso's fans, no one was more devoted than a twelve-year-old schoolgirl named Heather Noble. Born in Austria and adopted by an American couple who were stationed in Salzburg, Heather and her new family moved to Arlington, Virginia, before she turned two. After being stricken with polio as a young girl, Heather became lonely and withdrawn. She immersed herself in books about horses. Betrayed by her own legs, she was awe-struck by the spindly legs of the Thoroughbred and the speed they generated. Through the horses, she could envision what it was like to glide effortlessly over the ground with grace and power. After a while the horse books became her only interest, and she retreated further and further into her equine fantasy world.

Heather was watching a horse race on television one afternoon when something inexplicable happened. One of the horses appeared to look right through her television screen and deep into her soul. "Mother!" she screamed. "That horse looked at me. He looked right at me!"

That horse was Kelso. Whatever mystical connection was made that day brought Heather out of her make-believe world and into a real world filled with the same beauty she had discovered in her horse books. She began collecting everything she could find about Kelso, and she wrote to Kelso several times a week, sending him cardboard hearts, poems, and songs, some in the form of three-dimensional cards. She couldn't wait to share her excitement with her schoolmates. Television had brought a new generation of youngsters into the wondrous world of horses through gallant steeds such as Trigger, Champion, Silver, and Flicka. And, of course, there was the famous Mr. Ed, whose TV series had debuted January 5, 1961. If a horse could talk, why couldn't one communicate to a young girl through a television screen?

Heather told her schoolmates stories of this wonderful animal that had come into her life. Soon, she began making friends with other horse enthusiasts. As her mother said at the time, "Kelso is doing more for Heather than all the doctors and medicine put together."

Heather began corresponding regularly with four other young Kelso admirers — Joan Jaseinski, whom she had met at Aqueduct in 1962; Teri Purvis of Kingston, New York; Chris Ayers of Portland, Indiana; and Jill Cortwright of Albion, Michigan. In early 1963, Heather and her new friends started the Kelso Fan Club. There were no dues, just a common love and admiration for a gallant champion and all horses in general. Soon others came aboard. Membership eventually skyrocketed into the thousands. The club's *Kelsoland* newsletter grew from one or two pages to fifteen to twenty pages. Members included not only young horse lovers, but also owners, trainers, jockeys, and racing writers.

The heading on the newsletter read: "Kelso: Horse of Our Hearts Forever," followed by "Kelsoland. Kelsoland. A funful place to be. True friends meet with him there in heart and memory."

Within a year Heather became well known for her dedication to Kelso. She appeared on television and was interviewed in newspapers and magazines. When the Kelso Room opened at Laurel in 1965, displaying many of his trophies and paintings and other memorabilia, Heather served as hostess. Mrs. du Pont had tears in her eyes as they hugged and kissed. Heather and Teri Purvis then presented Mrs. du Pont with a gray-and-yellow blanket for Kelso. The blanket was hand embroidered and inscribed with numerous messages to their hero. The ultimate tribute for Heather occurred when Mrs. du Pont later named Kelso's half sister Heather Noble.

CHAPTER 9

The Times They Are A Changin'

As Kelso embarked on his six-year-old campaign, no one could have predicted that the age of innocence was nearing an end. Americans had gone through a brief, but frightening, prelude in October 1962 when the Cuban Missile Crisis spread fear across the nation. But President Kennedy helped resolve the ordeal, and the nation regained its equanimity. However, a sense of unrest was growing. By the end of 1963, Kennedy would be dead, and soon after young men all over the country would be thrust into war, while on the home front, the civil rights movement would heat up.

But in early 1963, Americans still retained their Hula Hoop and *Father Knows Best* mentality and found their pleasures in the purer and simpler things of life. And one of those pleasures was Kelso, a hero as pure and simple and enduring as the times in which he lived.

In January the unassuming hero was put on a van and sent down to Florida, where he would get an early start and point for the prestigious Widener Handicap at Hialeah.

Across the country an all-star cast of older horses was preparing to take center stage. In addition to the pesky Beau Purple, there was the cream of the three-year-old crop of '62: Jaipur and Ridan (in Florida), Kentucky Derby winner Decidedly and Crimson Satan (in California), Mongo (in Maryland), and Admiral's Voyage (in New York). All were expected to make an impact on the handicap division. Noticeable by his absence was Carry Back, who had been retired following his third-place finish in the Washington, D.C., International.

Shortly after arriving at Hialeah, Dickie Jenkins was approached by Charlie Eye, who worked for Ridan's trainer LeRoy Jolley. "Hey, Dickie, whatcha been doin' with that horse?" he asked.

"Just gallopin' him on the farm," Jenkins said. "Didn't really get much in him and he'll need a race."

That race was the seven-furlong Palm Beach Handicap on January 30, also the target for Ridan. Eye was confident Ridan could knock off the champ, the horse having already won a seven-furlong prep for the Palm Beach by five lengths in a swift 1:22 3/5.

"There ain't no way Kelso can beat Ridan going seven-eighths," Eye told Jenkins. Ridan was one of the fastest horses in the country, but he could carry it a distance, having won several top-class stakes at three and losing the Travers by a nose to Jaipur. With Jaipur also pointing for the Palm Beach, Kelso's six-year-old debut was certainly not going to be an easy spot, especially considering he had virtually no hard training for the race.

Held in high regard by the betting public, Ridan was made the overwhelming favorite at 3-5, with Kelso at 2-1 and Jaipur 9-2. Kelso was assigned top weight of 128 pounds, with Ridan and Jaipur both at 127. A fresh Kelso showed good speed out of the gate, dueling with Ridan and Jaipur through an opening quarter in :23 3/5. But Kelso's lack of conditioning took its toll, and he tired to finish fourth behind Ridan, who beat Jaipur by nearly four lengths in 1:22 4/5 over a fast but dull track.

The next stop on the road to the Widener was the

mile and one-eighth Seminole Handicap on February
9. Five days before the race Kelso worked a mile in
1:39 and galloped out a mile and one-eighth in 1:52
3/5. He was ready to take on Ridan and Jaipur. Also in
the field was Hitting Away, a wire-to-wire winner of
the nine-furlong Royal Palm Handicap two weeks earlier. The fans thought Ridan was Kelso's heir apparent,
and they made him the 6-5 favorite, with Kelso 2-1.
Kelso wasn't even the high weight, carrying 128 to
Ridan's 129. But the king was far from dead. Kelso settled in fourth, with Valenzuela tracking Ridan and
jockey Steve Brooks all the way. When Valenzuela
asked Kelso for his run on the final turn, the old warrior blew past Ridan with such force, Brooks said afterward, "He went by me so fast I got wind burn."

Kelso drew off to win by almost three lengths over
Ridan in 1:48 4/5. Jaipur faded to fourth after battling
on the lead with Hitting Away for almost seven furlongs.

The scene changed dramatically for the February 23
Widener. Ridan wrenched an ankle training for the
race, and Bert Mulholland wisely passed the race with
Jaipur. That left Kelso's old nemesis, Beau Purple, as
his main threat. But the Hobeau horse hadn't run since

his forty-length drubbing in the Washington, D.C., International the past November. Beau Purple had always been plagued with cracked heels and was prone to sore feet. Allen Jerkens hadn't liked the way Beau Purple was moving in the days following the International, and Jack Dreyfus had suggested sending the horse to the farm. "If he doesn't come around, we'll just breed him," he had told Jerkens.

Beau Purple eventually did come around, and Jerkens had the unenviable task of training him up to the mile and a quarter Widener off a three-month layoff.

Jerkens tried to get a prep race into Beau Purple before the Widener, but the colt kept splitting his heels open. Once Beau Purple's feet finally healed, Jerkens decided to work the horse hard and long to see if he was up to the grueling task of taking on Kelso without a prep. The Monday before the race Beau Purple went out and worked a mile and one-eighth in 1:49 3/5 in the pouring rain. Jerkens, who was never known for doing things by the book, then breezed him five furlongs in 1:01 the day before the race. He was now convinced Beau Purple was ready.

As for Kelso's Widener preparations, Hanford was making sure the gelding was staying sharp. On the Sunday before the race, Kelso worked a mile and one-eighth in 1:50 2/5 in the mud. On the gelding's daily training chart, Hanford wrote: "Galloped out in 2:04 3/5 in the mud and was held up last quarter. Best work and easiest I ever saw. Lost shoe at 1/2 (half-mile pole) or 3/8."

On paper the Widener appeared to be a two-horse race between Kelso and Beau Purple, but to win Beau Purple would need to burst out of the gate and try to steal the race on Kelso, as he had done twice before. But a surprise was in store for Beau Purple's rivals. When the entries came out, everyone was stunned to see Kilmoray listed in the field. Kilmoray was a six-furlong speedball owned by Dreyfus and trained by Jerkens. It made no sense. Why would Jerkens enter a speed horse who had no shot to win and could only prevent Beau Purple from getting the easy lead he needed?

As it turned out, it was Dreyfus' doing. He had the idea that by putting Kilmoray in the race, everyone would think they were going to send him to the lead instead of Beau Purple, and it would confuse Valenzuela. The main reason Dreyfus did it, however, was that he was upset at Hanford for saying that all Kelso had to do was run at Beau Purple early and he'd beat him. Dreyfus told Jerkens, "He's got three Horse of the Year titles; why does he have to knock our horse?"

Jerkens' instructions to John Rotz, on Kilmoray, were to get out of the gate, grab a hold of him, and take him back. Kilmoray was in the race just to give Hanford and Valenzuela something to think about. And that he did. If Kilmoray had drawn outside of Kelso, Hanford figured he would be no factor and the Hobeau connections probably wouldn't even run him. But if he drew inside Kelso, then Valenzuela would have to watch him before deciding what to do. Beau Purple drew the ideal rail spot, with Kilmoray drawing post four and Kelso post five.

From the moment the gates opened, the race turned into a disaster for Kelso, who was carrying 131 pounds, six more than Beau Purple. Boland shot to the lead with Beau Purple, while Valenzuela grabbed a tight hold of Kelso. Rotz did the same on Kilmoray. By the time Valenzuela realized that Kilmoray was not going anywhere but backward, Kelso was caught in a traffic jam, while Beau Purple had complete control of the race. The Hobeau horse skipped along through lethargic fractions of :24 3/5, :48 3/5, and 1:12 2/5, with Kelso back in fourth, almost a half-dozen lengths off the pace. By the time Valenzuela was able to get Kelso in full gear, the race was over and Kelso could only get up for second. Beau Purple won by two and a quarter lengths in 2:01 4/5, conquering Kelso for the third time.

Four days later Jerkens sent out G.H. Bostwick's Pocosaba to upset the 2-5 Cicada in the Black Helen Handicap. For Jerkins this was to be only the beginning. His legend would grow over the years with shocking upsets of superstars such as Secretariat (twice), Buckpasser, Forego, Riva Ridge, Skip Away, Numbered Account, and numerous other champions, earning him the nickname "the Giant Killer."

Soon after the Black Helen, Jerkens came down with rheumatic fever. While Jerkens was in the hospital, Beau Purple began having more setbacks, including a suspicious tendon. When Jerkens returned, Dreyfus asked him, "Is there any doubt in your mind that this horse is as good as before?" When Jerkens told him he had his doubts, Dreyfus simply said, "Send him home."

Kelso's thorn finally had been removed for good. Ahead of him was clear sailing. With Kelso allowed to run his own race, and Valenzuela and Hanford not having to keep changing strategy because of one horse, the champ had the rest of the season pretty much to himself, and went on to win eight consecutive stakes, dispelling any doubts that he was the same horse he'd been at three, four, and five. He started with the Gulfstream Park Handicap.

In the mile and a quarter race, he was lowered one pound to 130 and was giving away from sixteen to twenty pounds to his five overmatched opponents. With no pace in the race, Valenzuela sent Kelso up to engage Jay Fox right from the start. After a brief tussle through slow fractions, Kelso turned back the challenge of California invader Sensitivo, then drew off to win eased up by three and a quarter lengths.

The morning after the race, while Hanford and Mrs. du Pont relaxed on lawn chairs outside the barn, Jenkins was having a helluva time "keeping Kelso on the ground." The horse was bucking and jumping, obviously feeling no effects from the race. The $100,000 John B. Campbell Handicap, run March 23 at Bowie Race Course, was only a week away, and not in Kelso's plans, but when Jenkins told Hanford and Mrs. du Pont how good the horse was feeling, they decided to load him on a van and send him to Maryland.

The Campbell was not going to be an easy spot. Mongo, who had upset Carry Back in the previous year's Trenton Handicap, was primed and ready, following his easy three and a half-length victory in the mile and one-sixteenth Bowie Handicap. Shipping in from California was Crimson Satan, who had already won the Charles H. Strub and San Fernando stakes at Santa Anita and had finished second in the Santa Anita and San Antonio handicaps. Kelso also would have to drop back from a mile and a quarter to a mile and one-sixteenth.

Kelso was assigned 131 pounds, with Mongo carrying 128 and Crimson Satan 124 in the six-horse field. The fans made Kelso the 4-5 favorite, but there was plenty of support for Mongo at 8-5. It was longshot Gushing Wind who shot to the lead, opening up a three-length advantage. Mongo was in good position in third, with Kelso and Crimson Satan bringing up the rear. By the time they hit the quarter pole, Kelso had moved up to challenge Mongo, but Gushing Wind was still in front by three lengths. Mongo couldn't match strides with Kelso, who began cutting into Gushing Wind's lead. But the pacesetter, in receipt of fifteen pounds from Kelso, wouldn't give up without a fight. It was only until they were inside the sixteenth pole that Kelso was able to stick his head in front. He began to ease away as Crimson Satan launched his late bid. At the wire it was Kelso by three-quarters of a length over Crimson Satan, who just got up by a head to beat out Gushing Wind for second. The time of 1:43 was only two-fifths of a second off the track record.

After the John B. Campbell, Hanford and Mrs. du Pont came to a decision. Having changed course this year, starting early in Florida, they knew Kelso would have to be given a break at some point and with his hard effort in the Campbell, now seemed as good a time as any. His best races always came in the fall, and they couldn't expect the old boy to race under top weights starting in January and still be fresh for races like the Woodward, Gold Cup, and International.

Kelly had run thirty-eight times in his career, winning twenty-five of them. Instead of being pointed for the Metropolitan Handicap, as in the previous two years, Kelso was sent to Woodstock Farm, only a short drive from Bowie. He would unwind until June, then return to Hanford at Belmont Park and begin preparation for a summer and fall campaign.

His vacation at Woodstock was a tonic for the old warrior, as he indulged in chocolate ice cream, candy, and cake. Kelso had lost one of his canine buddies, Mickey, a short time earlier. Mickey, who had appeared with Kelso on the Hanfords' Christmas card in 1960 had gone blind, and there was nothing for the Hanfords to do but put him to sleep. At the farm, however, Kelso was reunited with Charlie Potatoes, who provided canine companionship virtually day and night.

Kelso demanded constant praise and attention from his owner, and Mrs. du Pont certainly obliged. He would nuzzle against her and seemed to enjoy, or at least accept, her hugs and kisses.

In the paddock before a race, however, she knew to keep her distance. Kelso had no time for amenities. He'd put on his game face and become dead serious.

When he lost, it was a "devastating spectacle," according to Mrs. du Pont, who said he would become "forlorn and ashamed of himself. No matter how much affection you lavish on him, it's impossible to console him."

But when he won, he was lovable and affectionate, and would nuzzle up to Mrs. du Pont and give a soft whinny, which was his way of asking for his lumps of sugar. "Oh, stop now!" Mrs. du Pont would say to him. "You're acting like a silly kitten. Of course, I know you won. What do you think I expected you to do?"

Kelso returned to the track to point for the June 19 Nassau County Stakes at a mile and one-eighth. His thin hoof walls had always been a concern to Hanford. Instead of equipping Kelso with the standard horseshoes with eight holes, he had the blacksmith create new holes in between each of the eight standard openings, giving Kelso's shoes sixteen holes. That way, each time he was re-shod, the nails would be driven into a different part of the hoof. Hanford also made sure he waited long periods of time between shoeings. He had Kelso shod four days before the Nassau County and would keep the same shoes on him for the July 4 Suburban Handicap.

Kelso was ready to pick up where he left off before his vacation. Under the allowance conditions of the Nassau County, Kelso had to carry high weight of 132 pounds, giving eighteen pounds to his four opponents. Kelso was sent off at 3-10, with only Garwol getting any play at 5-1. With the Suburban Handicap coming up, Hanford told Valenzuela to make sure he didn't win by too big a margin. Kelso took the lead at the head of the stretch, and Valenzuela had all he could do to throttle him down in the final eighth to win by a length and a half in 1:48 4/5. Despite being eased to a gallop, Kelso missed the track record by only three-fifths of a second.

The Fourth of July dawned sunny and warm, and even with the many outdoor alternatives, 52,136 fans showed up at Aqueduct to see their hero carry 133 pounds and concede from eighteen to twenty-three pounds to his six opponents, who included the Met Mile winner, Cyrano, and Saidam, coming off a mile overnight handicap score in 1:34 4/5. Bobby Ussery, on Cyrano, was allowed to set snail-like fractions of :48 4/5 and 1:13 1/5, with Kelso sitting in third, two lengths behind. After a mile in 1:38 1/5, Valenzuela asked Kelso for his run, and the gelding put Cyrano away, then opened a length and a half lead at the eighth pole. Saidam, in receipt of twenty-two pounds, came flying late, but Kelso had no problem holding him safe, winning by a length and a quarter. Despite the 133 pounds, Kelso closed his final quarter in a sizzling :23 1/5 to complete the mile and a quarter in a solid 2:01 4/5.

Instead of running Kelso back in the Monmouth Handicap or the Brooklyn, Hanford elected to wait for the Whitney at Saratoga, where Kelso would carry "only" 130 pounds under the allowance conditions. In Kelso's absence, Decidedly won the Monmouth Handicap over Mongo, and Cyrano wired his field in the Brooklyn under 113 pounds.

Neither of those two wanted any part of Kelso under the conditions of the Whitney. Kelso still had to give away thirteen to twenty pounds, but large weight concessions rarely fazed the old boy. Although he was rank early, fighting Valenzuela, Kelso made light work of the Whitney, winning by two and a half lengths, beating Saidam and Sunrise County, who was coming

off a nose defeat to Cyrano in the Brooklyn.

Labor Day in New York meant the mile and one-eighth Aqueduct Stakes. Under the race conditions, Kelso would have to shoulder 134 pounds and face some tough opponents, including Crimson Satan, fresh off a last-to-first victory in the Washington Park Handicap at Arlington, and new faces such as Decidedly and the brilliant three-year-old Candy Spots, winner of the Preakness, Santa Anita Derby, Florida Derby, American Derby, and Arlington Classic. Candy Spots, whose owner Rex Ellsworth, trainer Mesh Tenney, and jockey Bill Shoemaker were responsible for the great Swaps in 1955, had also run second in the Belmont Stakes and third as the solid favorite in the Kentucky Derby.

A massive holiday crowd of 71,876 packed Aqueduct, and Kelso didn't disappoint his loyal fans. He made light of his 134 pounds and drew off to a five and a half-length victory over Crimson Satan. Candy Spots, who had tracked the pace-setting Garwol for six furlongs, came back lame in his left front leg and was sent to Rex Ellsworth's ranch in California, ending a brilliant three-year-old season.

141

The Kelso juggernaut continued in his two favorite races, the Woodward and Jockey Club Gold Cup. There were few horses by now who wanted any part of Kelso. If they couldn't beat him with huge weight advantages, they surely weren't going to beat him at weight-for-age. But the Woodward did attract one very interesting horse, one who certainly was no stranger to Kelso.

In August, Jack Price brought Carry Back out of retirement, running him in the Buckeye Handicap at Randall Park, near Cleveland, Ohio. Carry Back ran well but couldn't catch the front-running Gushing Wind, who had given Kelso a bit of a tussle in the John B. Campbell. Price then put Carry Back on the grass at Atlantic City in a prep for the United Nations Handicap. He won easily by six lengths, but in the United Nations, under 127 pounds, he was unable to catch Mongo and Never Bend. That set Carry Back up for the Woodward and a return to the dirt. The three-year-old Never Bend, trained by Woody Stephens, also was entered. Owned by Harry Guggenheim's Cain Hoy Stable, Never Bend had won the Flamingo Stakes and was second to Chateaugay in the Kentucky Derby. Crimson Satan and Garwol rounded out the small, but talented, field.

One of those who did not contest the Woodward was Greentree Stable's three-year-old Outing Class, who had won the Dwyer and Saranac handicaps. When his trainer, John Gaver, was asked why he chose not to run, he answered emphatically, "Because I'm not convinced any horse belongs in that race except Kelso."

Kelso was the biggest draw New York racing had ever seen over such a long period of time, and his presence brought 50,234 fans to Aqueduct, which was the temporary home of the big fall stakes while the Belmont Park grandstand was being rebuilt after the original structure was condemned and torn down. Never Bend, under Bill Shoemaker, bounded to the front and set a sensible pace. Valenzuela, who had learned his lesson chasing Beau Purple, wasn't about to let the three-year-old out of his sight. He sat comfortably in second, and when Never Bend eased away to a three-length lead down the backstretch, Valenzuela went up to put pressure on him. Crimson Satan had already made his move and was in third, with Carry Back trying to keep up.

At the quarter pole Kelso collared Never Bend, who put up a good fight until the eighth pole. But Kelso, under no pressure whatsoever from Valenzuela, drew off on his own to win by three and a half lengths. Crimson Satan ran on well but couldn't catch Never Bend, while finishing six lengths ahead of Carry Back. Kelso's time of 2:00 4/5 was four-fifths of a second off Beau Purple's track record. It was amazing that a horse could close his last quarter in :24 1/5 while running so easily. It was in the weight-for-age races, under 126 pounds, that Kelso was really able to show his true brilliance and dominance over his rivals.

In the December issue of the *Kelsoland* newsletter, the account of the Woodward read: "People all around us were crying and pounding one another. When he came to the winner's circle, Kel knew exactly where he was and what he had done. His gift to us that day was one of eternal joy."

Kelso had won his third straight Woodward and would now try for his fourth straight Jockey Club Gold Cup. Although seven horses showed up, the race was a freebie for Kelso. None of those entered could even warm up the champ going two miles, and the 50,131 fans on hand sent him off at fifteen cents to the dollar. When Kelso had to steady between horses early, Valenzuela figured he'd better get him to the front. If he were to get Kelso beat, he probably would have to just keep on going, never to be seen again. After that worrisome moment, Valenzuela put Kelso on the lead and just let him roll along at his own leisure. Coming to the wire, Kelso had the field strung out over thirty lengths, as he cruised to a four-length victory in what was nothing more than a workout. His reliable shadows, Guadalcanal and Garwol, picked up their usual bits and pieces, finishing second and third, respectively.

Kelso was riding an eight-race winning streak, and all that was left for him was the elusive Washington, D.C., International. Twice he had run big races, and twice he had been beaten. The field included major group stakes winners from France, Ireland, Russia, Venezuela, Germany, and Hungary. For the third straight year Kelso had to hook up well before the stretch with a top-class American grass horse. This time it was Mongo. Kelso had handled Mongo on the dirt with little difficulty, and Valenzuela did not want to suffer the same fate he had the previous year, when he ran Kelso into the ground trying to match strides with Beau Purple. This time he was content to sit back in fourth, as Mongo cruised on the lead by three lengths. However, Mongo managed to get away with a :25 opening quarter, which left him a fresh horse when Valenzuela finally brought Kelso up to challenge.

Hanford was hoping Valenzuela would hook Mongo and try to go by him down the backstretch, as there were no Match IIs in this year's field. But after looking Mongo in the eye, Valenzuela allowed Kelso to sit just off his flank instead of going for the lead, as Hanford had hoped. Valenzuela then let Mongo open up by a length. When Kelso challenged, Mongo carried him wide on the turn. Kelso managed to pull to within a half-length, as the pair drew a dozen lengths clear of the others. But Mongo had a :23 4/5 final quarter left in him, and Kelso could not get any closer than a half-length. Once again Kelso had run his heart out at Laurel, only to be beaten. Valenzuela claimed foul against Mongo, and after deliberating for twenty-three minutes, the stewards allowed the result to stand.

The defeat, however, could not diminish what Kelso had accomplished in 1963. Not only had he won eight stakes in a row, but he also had won six consecutive stakes carrying 130 pounds or more. In five years of racing, Kelso had won thirty-one of his forty-five starts, while lugging 130 pounds or more fifteen times. His amazing feats in 1963 earned him his fourth straight Horse of the Year title. Racing fans couldn't remember what it was like not having Kelso around.

Eleven days after the International, the world changed forever with the assassination of President Kennedy. It was a time when heroes were in desperate need, and although Kelso was nearing his seventh birthday, he still had a few miracles left.

CHAPTER 10

Long Live The King

K elso was now seven years old. Although he was coming off one of the most successful campaigns of his career, he spent the first half of 1964 trying to re-ignite the flame that many felt finally was beginning to dim. It took him until September to find the old spark, but when he did, it set off a flood of emotions that moved many to tears and inspired veteran Turf writers to pen some of the most passionate and profound words ever written about a Thoroughbred.

The world, in 1964, was changing rapidly. On the night of February 9, the innocent music of the early six-ties began its rapid descent into oblivion when four mop-haired kids from England called the Beatles sent a wave of mass hysteria throughout the Ed Sullivan Theater. That hysteria would infiltrate culture and change not only music but also the way people looked

148

and the way they dressed. That August, American planes bombed North Vietnam for the first time, and a few days later the Gulf of Tonkin Resolution basically became a declaration of war. By October, China had exploded its first atomic bomb. The harmonious world of the fifties and early sixties was gone forever.

Kelso, in his own small way, provided a final link to happier and more peaceful times. But the year did not start off well for the four-time Horse of the Year. Mrs. du Pont was aware that Kelly was getting old and battle worn, and there was great trepidation every time he ran. She knew that if anything happened to her beloved horse during a race she would never forgive herself. Hanford would often say he didn't know how much longer Mrs. du Pont could bear to watch Kelso race because of her constant fear of his getting hurt.

Hanford, however, also was being overly protective of his aging hero. His wife, Millie, would often awake in the middle of the night, only to find Carl gone from the bed to be with Kelso. The old horse was colicking more often, about two to three times a week, but Dickie Jenkins would walk him, and he'd always come out of it.

Hollywood Park officials had desperately tried to get

Kelso to come out there that spring, and Hanford and Mrs. du Pont finally decided to accept their invitation. So Kelso, Jenkins, and Fitz boarded a plane and headed for California. During the flight the plane had mechanical problems and was forced to land in Denver. The weather was snowy and windy, and when the door to the plane opened, a blast of cold air greeted Kelso. When the door remained open, Jenkins had to cover the horse with a blanket. Finally, they landed in Los Angeles, but after arriving at Hollywood Park, Jenkins and Fitz could see that Kelso was not his usual self. There was no fire in his eye, and he was not eating well.

Hanford arrived a short time later and was concerned that Kelso was off his feed. Kelso's barn was near the track kitchen and a pole with a loudspeaker and siren attached. Every time an announcement blared over the loudspeaker, Kelso would dart toward the webbing of his stall and poke his head out to see what was going on. The constant announcements often interrupted his eating, and he would just pick at his feed, taking all day to eat.

Hanford was pointing Kelso for the seven-furlong

Los Angeles Handicap on May 23. Several days before the race Jenkins took Kelso out for a five-furlong spin, just to let him stretch a little in about 1:01 and change. But shortly after breaking off, one of the exercise riders, working a young, precocious filly, came charging up to Kelso "hootin' and hollerin." Jenkins grabbed hold of Kelso, but it was too late. The old boy took off after the filly with his mouth wide open and wound up working in a blazing :57 and change. He came back bucking and playing and all wound up. At feeding time he wouldn't eat. Jenkins held the jugs while they fed him intravenously. "This horse ain't gonna run a hoot," Jenkins told Hanford.

He was right. Between all his troubles and a rock-hard racetrack that he hated, Kelso turned in dull efforts in the Los Angeles Handicap and Californian Stakes. Jenkins, Hanford, and Mrs. du Pont were more upset over the fact that the California fans never got a chance to see the real Kelso.

A local reporter took a shot at Kelso, writing that he was strictly a New York horse and couldn't win west of the Hudson River. Jenkins was so incensed that when he got back to New York, he bought a box of

Whitman's Samplers chocolates. He removed the chocolates from the paper wrappers and replaced them with pieces of Kelso's excrement, then mailed the box to the reporter, signed "From Kelso." Word got back to Jenkins that the reporter actually got a kick out of it.

When Kelso returned home, Hanford wasted no time in looking for a race to get him back on the right track. He found a mile and one-eighth overnight handicap on June 25, nineteen days after the Californian. Despite Kelso's two defeats, and being seven years old, Tommy Trotter still piled 136 pounds on Kelso. As the race drew near, no one could find Valenzuela. "I gotta get somebody to ride this horse," Hanford told Jenkins.

"You found him," Jenkins said. "I can tie a damn knot in my ass and win on him. If I can go over and get my license, I guarantee you I'll win on him."

The expression on Hanford's face was all Jenkins needed to see that this was a futile gesture. Valenzuela finally showed up and piloted Kelso to a length and a quarter victory over Tropical Breeze, who was in receipt of twenty-two pounds from Kelso. "Well, we ain't dead yet, anyhow," Hanford told a reporter. The old warrior came back huffing and puffing after nine furlongs in a tepid 1:50. This would be Kelso's last victory for two months.

Kelso ran back nine days later in the Suburban Handicap, with Trotter being more lenient, assigning him "just" 131 pounds. The morning of the race, Kelso colicked again, and Jenkins had to walk him out of it. After settling that crisis, Jenkins went across the street to Doles, a popular bar that served breakfast in the back. As he was wolfing down a ham and egg sandwich, a friend of his, Zeke Badgett, who was an assistant to Woody Stephens, came over and said, "We got this horse in today named Iron Peg who is one fast sonofabitch."

Iron Peg, owned by Captain Harry Guggenheim, was a four-year-old who had been sent to England, where he failed to win in five starts at three, although he did run third in a minor stakes. Returned to America, he broke his maiden by seven lengths before winning a six-furlong allowance race by six lengths in a blazing 1:09 2/5. In his last start before the Suburban, he stretched out to a mile in allowance company, winning by thirteen lengths in 1:34 3/5.

Also contesting the Suburban were Met Mile winner Olden Times, who had won impressively in 1:34 2/5, and Massachusetts Handicap winner Smart. Kelso was favored at 6-5 with Iron Peg, in with only 116 pounds, at 8-5.

Olden Times set the pace, with Iron Peg tracking him, and Kelso three lengths farther back in third. Iron Peg took over after turning for home, and Kelso charged up fast inside the eighth pole to pull on even terms. Up in the stands a hardened, veteran horseman shouted uncharacteristically, "Old man! Old man! Jesus, let the old man win!" But Iron Peg kept finding more and held off the champ to win by a head.

When Kelso's closing bid again fell short two weeks later in the Monmouth Handicap, many felt the champ had seen his best days and was nearing the end of his career. He had turned in a good effort at Monmouth, finishing well clear of Gun Bow and Olden Times, but just couldn't get past Mongo, losing by a neck under 130 pounds. Kelso was back a week later in the Brooklyn Handicap, again under 130 pounds. This time, however, he was never in the race, finishing a well-beaten fifth behind Gun Bow, who romped by twelve lengths, setting a track record of 1:59 3/5. Gun

Bow had become the first horse in the history of New York racing to break 2:00 for a mile and a quarter.

What no one knew, however, was that Kelso had come down with another case of colic that morning and never was able to settle down. Walking to the paddock, he was so wound up he cow-kicked constantly.

"We better tell Carl," Fitz said to Jenkins.

"Well, first let's see what he does when he gets over there," Jenkins replied.

When Kelso still was on edge and not acting right, Jenkins told Hanford. The horse had always managed to come out of it, and Hanford felt he would calm down once he jogged. But Kelso never ran a lick. Also going unnoticed, except by Valenzuela, was Kelso hitting his head on the starting gate at the break, which left a golf ball-sized knot just under his forelock. Most observers were convinced they were witnessing the end of the Kelso era.

As July gave way to August, Hanford decided Kelso needed a prep for the September 7 Aqueduct Handicap, and he chose a mile and one-eighth allowance race on the grass at Saratoga. Kelso got in with only 118 pounds and won easily, setting a course record of 1:46 3/5. That set him up for a rematch with Gun Bow.

The four-year-old Gun Bow had gotten his season off to a strong start with a twelve-length victory in the mile and a quarter Charles H. Strub Stakes in 1:59 4/5 and went on to score brilliant victories in the Gulfstream Park Handicap, San Fernando Stakes, and San Antonio Handicap for trainer Eddie Neloy. His breeder, Elizabeth Arden Graham, had sold him to Harry Albert and Mrs. John Stanley of Gedney Farms for $125,000 in December 1963, in a deal that also included the promising juvenile Gun Boat. Eight months later Mrs. Graham bought back 10 percent of the horse for $100,000.

Following his spectacular triumph in the Brooklyn, Gun Bow won the Whitney by ten lengths and the Washington Handicap at Arlington Park by two lengths in the slop, carrying 132 pounds. It looked certain the torch had been passed. Gun Bow was on the verge of taking the throne that Kelso had occupied since Gun Bow was a foal running around the fields of Mrs. Graham's Maine Chance Farm in Kentucky.

The Aqueduct Stakes was to be Gun Bow's *coup de*

grace. Both horses carried 128 pounds, and only three others dared to challenge racing's two titans. An enthusiastic Labor Day crowd of 65,066 showed up on a warm, seventy-five-degree day under clear skies. Red Smith, noted columnist for the *New York Times*, wrote what everyone had been thinking and hoping. "Some fear that the hour grows late for Kelso, yet autumn racing seems to be his deep-dish pie."

Kelso was the last horse to enter the paddock. As soon as the crowd lining the rail saw the plain brown horse with the familiar yellow ribbon tied to his forelock, they gave him a rousing welcome.

The anticipation was high. Was a new king about to be crowned? "Well, this is the moment of truth," said John Gaines of Gainesway Farm, who had recently syndicated Gun Bow for one million dollars. Milo Valenzuela walked into the paddock and put his arm on Mrs. du Pont's shoulder, as if to reassure her. Mrs. du Pont asked him about strategy against a speed horse like Gun Bow, and all Valenzuela could say was, "We can't run with him."

Hanford came over after saddling Kelso and told Valenzuela to go after Gun Bow if no one else did, a chore easier said than done. When someone came over and wished Mrs. du Pont luck, she replied, "Thank you, but we'll need more than that. Gun Bow is a wonderful colt. We'll need the kind of horse Kelso really is to beat him."

When Kelso walked on to the track, the crowd continued to pay tribute to their longtime hero. Red Smith wrote: "As Kelso moved up past the grandstand, rattling applause followed him like hailstone on the roof."

But the tote board contradicted the sentimental outpour. Gun Bow was the overwhelming 1-2 favorite, with Kelso at 2-1. At the start any thoughts Valenzuela had of running with Gun Bow quickly were gone. Walter Blum gunned the Gedney Farm colt to the front and immediately opened a four-length lead through an opening quarter in :23 1/5. After a half in a solid :46 3/5, Gun Bow had increased his lead to five lengths. Kelso was trying to stay within striking range in second, well clear of Saidam, Delta Judge, and Uppercut.

Leaving the backstretch, Valenzuela urged Kelso on, and the aging gelding began cutting into Gun Bow's lead. As they passed the three-eighths pole after three-quarters in 1:10 4/5, Kelso had whittled Gun Bow's lead down to a length and a half. He kept coming, as Blum, sensing the danger closing in on him, started rousing Gun Bow. "Look him in the eye, Kelly! Look him in the eye!" someone shouted from the grandstand.

Turning for home, Kelso was now on even terms with Gun Bow, as the crowd rose to its feet. The noise was deafening. Kelso stuck his head in front, then his neck. At the eighth pole, he was a half-length in front. But Gun Bow kept battling back. The more Gun Bow found, the more Kelso found. *Daily Racing Form*'s Charles Hatton wrote: "In the final desperate sixteenth, they went at one another with the fury of wounded tigers."

No matter how hard Gun Bow came back at him, Kelso would not let him get closer than his saddlecloth. The shouts from the crowd pleaded for Kelso to hold on. "Come on, Kelso!" "Go get him, Kelly!" And those were the fans who had bet on Gun Bow. At the finish it was Kelso by three-quarters of a length. The time of 1:48 3/5 was just two-fifths of a second off the track record. It was another six lengths back to Saidam in third.

The Aqueduct grandstand shook like never before. Perfect strangers hugged one another. Hatton described the scene as a "Roman triumph," and added that, "It is doubtful if anything quite so moving had been seen on a (New York) track since the origins of the sport in America."

Mrs. du Pont was overcome with emotion and couldn't hold back the tears. She raced to the winner's circle and kissed Kelso, then Valenzuela, then Dave Carnaghan of the New York Racing Association, then a photographer who happened to be standing nearby. When John Galbreath presented her with the trophy, she kissed him as well. She looked up at the crowd, and engulfed by their cheers, said, "They really do love him." Then, she kept asking, "Could you believe it? I couldn't believe it. I ran every inch with Kelso down the stretch."

John Hay Whitney, owner of the famed Greentree Stable, said, "I don't think I've ever had a greater thrill on the racetrack."

Red Smith wrote: "As a horse race ends, there is one last cry, then silence for a moment before the babbling begins. This time the silence didn't fall. For a while it seemed it never would."

But it was Jack Mann, writing in the New York *Herald Tribune*, who said it best: "It was Lou Gehrig's farewell at Yankee Stadium and Willie Mays' return to

New York. It was sincere noise, a tribute to a champion who wouldn't let himself be beaten, even by time."

When the emotions finally did subside, it was back to reality and another showdown with a revenge-seeking Gun Bow in the Woodward Stakes. A victory by the four-year-old would once again give him the advantage in his quest to dethrone Kelso. With the prospect of another epic battle, 51,108 showed up at Aqueduct on September 28. The only other horse of note in the five-horse field was Rokeby Stable's Quadrangle, who in June had spoiled Kentucky Derby and Preakness winner Northern Dancer's attempt to sweep the Triple Crown by winning the Belmont Stakes. He had followed that up with victories in the Dwyer Handicap and Travers Stakes.

This time Kelso was back to his familiar role as favorite, as the fans sent him off at 4-5, with Gun Bow at 7-5. With no one to run with Gun Bow, Valenzuela had no choice but to get Kelso into the race early. Kelso broke like a bullet, and Valenzuela hustled him to the lead. This was not where Valenzuela expected to be, so he grabbed hold of Kelso, as Gun Bow shot past him. Unlike the Aqueduct, Blum and Gun Bow were allowed to set easy fractions. Valenzuela had Kelso only a length or two back, but with a half in :48 1/5 and three-quarters in 1:12 1/5, Gun Bow was going to be tougher to crack this time.

Valenzuela waited until he was midway on the far turn before unleashing his move. Kelso, as he had done in the Aqueduct, gained a short lead after turning into the stretch, while Quadrangle moved up menacingly along the rail, trying to catch the top two napping. Kelso increased his margin to a neck, but this time Gun Bow had more left in the tank. Kelso, in uncharacteristic fashion, began to lug in, costing him valuable momentum and allowing Gun Bow back in the fight. Once again the fans went wild as they were treated to another titanic battle.

With Valenzuela having to drag Kelso back off Gun Bow, he wasn't able to ride the horse properly and drive him to the wire. Gun Bow fought back to reach even terms, as the pair eyeballed each other every step of the final furlong. Just as Gun Bow stuck his head in front, Kelso battled back. The two bobbing heads hit the wire together, and it was left to the camera to separate them. After an excruciatingly long wait, Gun

Bow's number went up. The finish was so close, many to this day still look at the photo and insist it was a dead-heat.

To the credit of Hanford and Mrs. du Pont, they never once in Kelso's career resorted to using a "rabbit," or pacesetter, despite Kelly's having to face, and concede weight to, several top-class frontrunners, often the only speed in small fields. Who knows how many more races Kelso might have won had they sent out another horse to soften up Beau Purple or Gun Bow or Mongo?

Although the photo didn't go Kelso's way, the battle for Horse of the Year still was not over. Instead of facing Kelso in the October 31 Jockey Club Gold Cup, where the old gelding was seemingly invincible, Neloy opted for the Man o' War Stakes for Gun Bow a week earlier. The mile and five-eighths turf race would also serve as a prep for the Washington, D.C., International, a race in which Kelso had been far from invincible.

Gun Bow was made the 3-5 favorite in the Man o' War but was cooked in a speed duel with the quick Cedar Key. The Laurel Turf Cup winner, Turbo Jet II, engaged Gun Bow at the head of the stretch before opening a clear lead. Gun Bow fought back again, but his bid fell three-quarters of a length short. If Kelso could dominate his field in the two-mile Jockey Club Gold Cup, it would set up a final confrontation with Gun Bow in the International to decide Horse of the Year once and for all.

The Gold Cup wasn't shaping up as a typical walk in the park for Kelso. He would have to contend with the distance-loving Quadrangle and a new face, Harbor View Farm's indefatigable little three-year-old Roman Brother, who had won six stakes in 1964, including the American Derby, Jersey Derby, New Hampshire Sweepstakes, and Discovery Handicap, as well as finishing second to Quadrangle in the Belmont Stakes. In their previous start, the mile and five-eighths Lawrence Realization, Quadrangle and Roman Brother had hooked up in another marathon duel, with Quadrangle just holding off Roman Brother to win by a neck.

The morning of the race, Kelso colicked yet again. When Fitz fed him that morning, Kelso wouldn't go near the tub. "This sonofabitch is sick," Jenkins said to Fitz. Kelso was given an enema and treated with whatever medication was permissible on race day. Jenkins walked him all morning. It was now eleven o'clock and the van from Belmont was due to leave for Aqueduct in about an hour.

Shortly before departing, Jenkins went in Kelso's stall to tie the ribbon to the gelding's forelock. As he was tying it, he looked up and saw that Kelso had his head up and was staring out the stall door "with his eyes bulging right out of his head." He knew then the horse was ready to do something big.

When the van arrived, Jenkins took a handful of alfalfa, went inside and tossed it in the corner, just to see if Kelso would go over and eat it. If he did, then he'd know he was feeling his old self. Sure enough, Kelso walked to the back of the van and started picking on the alfalfa.

Then he went out and picked on Quadrangle and Roman Brother. He broke the race open after a mile and a half and left the two three-year-olds floundering behind him. The crowd, seeing Kelso draw off with the utmost ease, sensed they were watching something special. And the cheers once again erupted.

David Alexander wrote in the *Thoroughbred Record*: "First, there was a sudden, almost absolute silence among the thousands. Then, as if they were acting on cue, 102,000 hands belonging to 51,000 persons began to clap. It was an awesome sound, one I have never heard before in the United States. It was applause in unison, hands beating rhythmically to Kelso's rhythmic stride."

Kelso drew off with every one of those rhythmic strides, as Valenzuela just sat wrapped up on him. What was most amazing was that, despite winning with such ridiculous ease by five and a half lengths over Roman Brother, Kelso was able to run the two miles in 3:19 1/5, breaking his own track and American record. After forty years the record still stands.

Alexander called it a "matchless experience of watching a perfect creature perform at the peak of its perfection, of seeing a living thing move down the stretch with the cadenced assurance of a Beethoven symphony." Alexander, who had been covering racing for four decades, went on to call Kelso "the greatest racehorse the American turf has ever known."

Not only had Kelso broken his own record, he had won his fifth Jockey Club Gold Cup, a feat unprecedented in racing history, and passed Round Table as the

all-time leading money-winner with earnings of
$1,803,362.

Now, all that stood between Kelso and a fifth Horse
of the Year title was Gun Bow and a mile and a half
stretch of Laurel turf that had proven his downfall on
three previous occasions.

Immediately after the Gold Cup Mrs. du Pont
announced that the November 11 International would
be Kelso's last race, adding to the emotional impact of
the event.

The day before the race Hanford had Jenkins work
Kelso a stiff half-mile. He wanted to make sure he
infused enough speed in the old boy to allow him to
hook Gun Bow early on. Kelso sizzled the four furlongs
in :46 1/5. When someone with a stopwatch relayed
the time to a group of reporters, one British scribe
uttered, "I say, that's rather fast for grass, isn't it?"

When entries were drawn for the race, Gun Bow
drew post one, which sent his co-owner, Harry Albert,
leaping in the air. "Perfect!" he shouted. "Perfect!
Perfect!"

After three heartbreaking defeats Mrs. du Pont felt
there was a jinx surrounding the International and was

just waiting for something to go wrong. When she heard that Gun Bow had drawn the rail, she said, "I knew it. It's always something in the International. If only we could have been inside of Gun Bow."

A bright spot for Mrs. du Pont was meeting Heather Noble for the first time. Heather showed up dressed in Bohemia Stable's gray and yellow colors. She also was wearing an assortment of Kelso badges and carried a home-made pennant on which was inscribed: "Win, lose or draw, I love you Kelso." Mrs. du Pont introduced Heather to sportswriters, society figures, racing officials, and some of the leading horsemen in the country, making it a memorable day for the teenager. She also sat with Mrs. du Pont in the du Pont box for several races before leaving to rejoin her mother. As she began walking away, she told Mrs. du Pont, "Kelly's going to win today, I just know it."

Walking in line to the special saddling area set up in the infield, Kelso was the only horse not wearing his International blanket. The champ was not fond of heavy clothing, and Fitz carried the blanket in his arm as Kelso flexed his muscles before the huge crowd of 37,800, including a number of international dignitaries. For the race Kelso wore the same saddle cloth Mrs. du Pont's daughter, Lana, had used in the Olympics. In the post parade Valenzuela could sense that Kelso was "high." Higher than he'd ever felt him. The horse was so up that Valenzuela was afraid he might wheel at the tape, so he kept a tight hold of him to prevent him from galloping off.

The International drew a field of eight, representing seven countries. Heading the invaders were the Russian sensation Aniline, unbeaten in 1964; Irish St. Leger winner Biscayne II; French Oaks winner Belle Sicambre; and the Gran Premio del Jockey Club winner Veronese II, from Italy.

The Laurel turf course was hard following a long drought, and a course record was a distinct possibility. Kelso was made the 6-5 favorite, with Gun Bow at 3-2. Only Italy's Veronese II, at 5-1, received any play. What it basically boiled down to was a match race between Kelso and Gun Bow.

When the tape was lifted, Gun Bow quickly burst clear, as Valenzuela hustled Kelso to take up second position. After an opening quarter in :24, Gun Bow was cruising in front by three lengths, and Kelso had a two and a half-length advantage on Biscayne II and Belle Sicambre. As they came past the stands for the first time, Gun Bow was flying through a half in :46 4/5, while increasing his lead to four lengths. That's the way it remained around the turn and down the backstretch. The crowd anxiously awaited the imminent explosion, when Valenzuela would light the fuse on Kelso. Gun Bow had drilled the six furlongs in 1:10 2/5, faster than most sprints.

Passing the five-eighths pole, Kelso began to close in for the kill, just waiting for Valenzuela to give him the signal. Up in the stands someone stood and shouted, "Now, Milo, now!" As if on cue, Valenzuela began scrubbing on Kelso, and the champ hooked Gun Bow after a torrid mile in 1:34 4/5. Walter Blum still had a good hold of Gun Bow, while Valenzuela was already driving Kelso, vigorously hand-riding him. Gun Bow still had something left and as the pair battled around the final turn, Gun Bow came out slightly into Kelso, who returned the favor.

They hit the quarter pole in 2:00 flat, with Kelso easing away from his rival by a half-length. Then, in a flash, it was over. Kelso had no more desire to entertain Gun Bow, and he quickly opened up by two lengths, then three. The crowd stood in unison and began its deafening tribute to the old warrior. Valenzuela merely hand-rode Kelso the rest of the way, as he coasted home by four and a half lengths. With a brilliant final quarter in :23 4/5, Kelso stopped the timer at 2:23 4/5, knocking one and two-fifths seconds off the course record and three-fifths of a second off the American record for a mile and a half. No horse in the Western Hemisphere had ever run that fast — on grass or dirt. The only horse ever to run a faster mile and a half was the three-year-old English colt, The Bastard, who went in 2:23 over Newmarket's undulating course in 1929.

Eddie Blind, Laurel's starter, was watching the race from the winner's circle, and when he looked up and saw the time, he said, "Horses can't run that fast."

Mrs. du Pont raced down to the winner's circle. In another section of the stands, Heather Noble was overcome with emotion. Then came the announcement that turned the bedlam into a foreboding hush: "Ladies and gentleman, please hold all tickets. There has been an objection by the rider of Gun Bow against the winner."

"Oh, no!" cried Mrs. du Pont, who couldn't help but think of the International jinx. Still, she maintained a smile on her face. When photographers asked her to turn for a picture, she obliged, unable to hide the tears in her eyes. Her daughter, Lana, also became misty-eyed, and said to no one in particular, "If it was a nose or a neck or something like that, but can they take his number down when he won by so much?"

Blind came over to congratulate Mrs. du Pont, who was staring at the flashing numbers on the tote board with her fingers crossed. "Not yet," she told him.

Then, after ten agonizing minutes, the numbers stopped flashing. The result stood. Kelso had gone out a winner, and in all likelihood had nailed down his fifth Horse of the Year title, while boosting his earnings to $1,893,362.

After the race, reporters converged on Blum to ask him about claiming foul. "Don't get me wrong," he said. "I couldn't have won, even if Kelso hadn't come in on me, but I owed it to the owners and the public to at least have the stewards look at the film. Maybe I'm some kind of a nut, but I honestly feel that Kelso goes out on the track with the will to win. That makes him dig in like no other horse. He's got a heart as big as himself. He knows what he's doing and he likes what he's doing. That's what makes him so great."

Even Eddie Arcaro, who attended the race, was in awe of his old partner. "I've never seen a horse like him," he said. "I thought he was great when I had him, but today he was the greatest."

On the winner's platform, when the band struck up "The Star Spangled Banner," Mrs. du Pont could no longer hold back the tears. Later, as she sipped champagne in the directors' room, she again said that Kelso's racing days likely were over. As the late autumn sun set, the crowd slowly filed out of Laurel, including an emotionally drained Heather Noble.

David Alexander concluded his wrap-up of the day's events by writing: "When the official sign was finally posted, a young girl in a yellow skirt and sweater and a perky yellow hat sank down in her box seat, breathless, voiceless, and too tired to hold her proud pennant aloft.

"Going to Heaven for a day can be an exhausting experience."

KELSO

CHAPTER 11

The End Of An Era

W as Kelso retired or not? No one had a clue. After the International, he had returned to Woodstock Farm and was living in the lap of luxury. By January 1965 the eight-year-old gelding had already entertained more than two hundred visitors, greeting them from his large stall, outside of which were four metal American flags from the International fastened to the wall.

Kelso had just been voted Horse of the Year for the fifth consecutive year, beating out archrival Gun Bow for the honor. With retirement still up in the air, the champ's only seemingly definite plan that year was making charitable appearances at U.S. and Canadian racetracks with proceeds donated to various equine research projects conducted by the Grayson Foundation (now the Grayson-Jockey Club Research

Foundation) and New Bolton Center of the University of Pennsylvania.

But as winter drew to an end, Kelso was starting to get antsy. There still was plenty of action left in the old boy. Hanford had expressed his wish to keep Kelso in training, saying the gelding was in such good condition it would be a shame to stop on him. In addition, Mrs. du Pont was receiving hundreds of letters a week from fans of all ages, begging her not to retire Kelso. As she always did, Mrs. du Pont and her secretary, Gertrude Jackson, answered every letter, whether it was sent to Mrs. du Pont or Kelso. Even Claiborne Farm's Bull Hancock commented that Kelso should be given the opportunity to become racing's first two million dollar earner.

Still, Mrs. du Pont would not commit her beloved gelding to another year of racing. Instead, she concentrated only on Kelso's appearances, one of which was at Keeneland Race Course on April 20. He was accompanied by Charlie Potatoes, who as usual watched over his buddy day and night, barking at anyone who got too close. Kelso was paraded on the track after the sixth race and then headed back to the barn. "Just look at him," Fitz said to some visitors. "His coat is nice and healthy and he's sound as a dollar...one helluva horse."

A month earlier, Kelso had visited Laurel to begin his mini charity tour, which included stops at Churchill Downs and Delaware Park, as well as Keeneland. With letters still pouring in daily and Kelso apparently enjoying his days back at the racetrack, Mrs. du Pont finally announced that the champ would return for an eight-year-old campaign. He rejoined Hanford's stable and appeared to relish his return to the racetrack. It was well into June, and there weren't many spots available for Kelso's first start. Hanford found a six-furlong allowance race at Monmouth Park on June 29. Although Kelso finished third, his furious late charge from eighth coming up a half-length short, it still was an excellent effort considering the distance and the seven and a half-month layoff. With Valenzuela busy riding in California, Kelso was ridden on this day by Beau Purple's old rider, Bill Boland, who was the first jockey other than Valenzuela to ride the champ since September 1962.

Hanford ran him back eleven days later under 130 pounds in the mile and one-sixteenth Diamond State Handicap at Delaware Park, and Kelso had an easy time, winning by three and a quarter lengths, missing the track record by three-fifths of a second. That set him up for the Brooklyn Handicap two weeks later and his first test against quality horses. Burdened with 132 pounds, Kelso had to give eleven pounds to Roman Brother, Quadrangle, and the red-hot Pia Star, winner of the Suburban Handicap and of the Equipoise Mile in a blazing 1:33 1/5, equaling the world record. To complicate matters, a heavy blanket of heat and humidity enveloped the Northeast, making for unbearable conditions.

When Fitz led Kelso into the paddock, a thunderous round of applause erupted from the crowd of 49,028. Cameras clicked and people along the railed shouted their support. Among them was Heather Noble, now fifteen years old, who found a spot right up against the rail and proudly waved her Kelsoland banner. While standing there, she signed up six new members to the Kelso Fan Club.

But the fairy tale return didn't go as planned. Pia Star ran another powerful race on the front end to defeat Roman Brother in a sharp 2:00 3/5. Kelso made a bold move on the turn and had the crowd on its feet, but he couldn't sustain it in the heat and humidity, especially under that much weight, and had to settle for third. The old boy had given it his all, and no one could be disappointed under the circumstances.

Two weeks later Kelso was back in the August 7 Whitney Stakes, under 130 pounds, this time conceding only three pounds to Pia Star under the allowance conditions. The morning of the race Dickie Jenkins was in Louie's Kitchen on the Saratoga backstretch when trainer George Poole walked in. Poole, a former assistant to Greentree trainer John Gaver, yelled over to Jenkins, "Hey, Dickie, when are you all gonna retire that old fart?"

"Hell, this old sucker still wants to run," Jenkins answered.

"Well, Greentree's got one in today, and he ain't gonna beat him," he said.

Poole was referring to Malicious, the Nassau County Stakes winner who was in the Whitney with a feathery 114 pounds.

In the tree-lined saddling area the crowd gathered six and seven deep. The Spa had not seen anything like it since Native Dancer returned there in 1953 to win the

Travers and remain undefeated at the track. Among those in attendance was The Right Reverend Arthur McKinstry, retired Episcopal bishop of Delaware who had officiated at the marriage of then President Lyndon B. Johnson and Lady Bird Johnson. At the thirtieth wedding anniversary party of President and Mrs. Johnson, a reporter asked the bishop if the cleric had any other claim to fame. He replied, "Well, among my friends in Wilmington I am casually spoken of as the private chaplain for the great racehorse Kelso."

The reporter asked, "Do you mean to say that you direct heavenly words to God on behalf of a race-horse?"

"I don't have to," the bishop replied. "Let's just say I sit there with my fingers crossed and hope a little. Actually, I get so nervous when Kelso runs that I try to recite the Greek alphabet backward to take my mind off things."

The bishop had every right to be nervous on this day. When Jenkins, aboard a pony, led Kelso to the gate, the horse turned his head slightly and looked right at him with little life in his eyes. As they approached the starting gate, the assistant starter grabbed Kelso's bridle to lead him into the gate and told Jenkins, "I think he's gonna get beat today, Dickie."

Jenkins jogged off to watch the race, hoping the man was wrong. Malicious, pulling sixteen pounds from Kelso, shot to the early lead and set moderate fractions of :23 2/5, :47 1/5, and 1:11 1/5. Kelso, the 6-5 favorite with the sentimental Saratoga crowd, was back in fourth in the five-horse field, five lengths off the pace. George D. Widener's Crewman took a run at Malicious, but quickly retreated. Pia Star was in striking range in third, but was unable to make up any ground. It was another three lengths back to Kelso, who was going nowhere. Jenkins finally conceded it wasn't his day. In the stands Hanford wondered, "What's wrong with him?"

Suddenly, Kelso seemed to rouse from a sound sleep. Valenzuela brought him off the rail and went to a series of left-handed whips. Malicious was still two and a half lengths in front passing the eighth pole, but Kelso was relentless as he bore down on him, just as he had against All Hands in the 1961 Met Mile when the reigning Horse of the Year had been a sprightly four-year-old. Now, it was all heart pushing those eight-year-old legs. Everyone knew it was going to be close. Kelso kept coming, driven by sheer will. He gave one final surge and stuck his nose in front right on the wire. It was six lengths back to Pia Star in third. Kelso returned to a hero's welcome. Even the hardened Dickie Jenkins, sitting atop the pony, was moved to tears.

A month later Kelso embarked on another autumn bid for Horse of the Year. He was even-money against Malicious, Roman Brother, Pluck, and Hill Rise in the Aqueduct Stakes, again under 130 pounds. But it was apparent from the start that Kelso had little interest in the race. His colic had been acting up again, and whether that had any bearing on his performance, he never was in the race, finishing a well-beaten fourth behind Malicious, Pluck, and Roman Brother. The Stymie Handicap on September 22 would determine whether the Aqueduct was an aberration or whether Kelso finally had reached the end.

Carrying 128 pounds, Kelso merely toyed with his five opponents, winning the mile and a quarter race by eight lengths. With the Horse of the Year title still wide open, there was plenty of time for Kelso to stage another late-season rally. But it was a short-lived dream. In the winner's circle, as Kelly posed for his picture, Jenkins noticed that the gelding had his left eye closed. When they returned to the barn, the horse's eye was as "white as a golf ball," according to Jenkins. Kelso's left orb had been severely damaged after apparently getting struck by a clod of dirt. As the condition of the eye worsened, there was fear he would lose the eye. Jenkins and Fitz had to take turns sitting by Kelso's side day and night, holding on to the shank and making sure he didn't rub the eye against something.

The eye healed after a week, and Kelso was sent back to Woodstock to recuperate, as Roman Brother went on to be named Horse of the Year, ending one of the most remarkable championship runs in sports history. One postcard sent to him was addressed to "King Kelso" and read: "Rest up, old fella. Your fans don't care about Horse of the Year, only about you. The people are with you. You are still the champ. There might be a new crown prince, but never another King!"

When Kelso once again began to get caught up in the lure of the racetrack the following year, Mrs. du Pont decided to give him one more chance. He still needed less than $23,000 to become the first horse ever to crack the two million dollar mark in earnings. He returned on March 2, 1966, at the age of nine but could manage only a fast-closing fourth in a six-furlong allowance race at Hialeah.

One morning, soon after, Kelso went out for a mile work and, after breaking into his gallop, ran up behind a string of Calumet Farm two-year-olds. One of them ducked to the outside, and Kelso was forced to slam on the brakes. He began to slide and took an awkward step. Jenkins noticed the old gelding was nodding his head after that, signifying something was bothering him, and jogged him instead of working him. When he felt Kelso take a bad step, he quickly pulled him up. Hanford, who was sitting on his pony watching the work, asked what happened, and Jenkins told him, "Man, I almost ran into the ass of that damn horse out there. This horse ain't right."

By the time Kelso returned to the barn, he was dead lame. Doc Harthill was at Hialeah to tend to Darby Dan Farm's three-year-old sensation, Graustark, and he came over to Hanford's barn and examined Kelso. X-rays revealed a fracture of the tip of the sesamoid.

Kelso was flown home to Woodstock Farm to recuperate, this time for good. He was retired with thirty-nine victories from sixty-three starts and record earnings of $1,977,896. After seven years, racing fans would have to get used to Saturdays without Kelso. It was like Metropolis without Superman. But other superstars would come along, such as Buckpasser, Damascus, Dr. Fager, and Arts and Letters, as the now-turbulent sixties drew to an end. All that was left of Kelso was the memory of a plain brown horse, decked out in yellow and gray, who once seemed eternal and who provided the nation with a kind of stability it would never see again.

Shortly after arriving at Woodstock, Kelso received a paddock buddy to keep him company and help him unwind from track life. Mrs. du Pont decided to team Kelso with a big, old hunter named Spray, who towered over the petite gelding. Kelso was placed in a paddock with Spray, and Mrs. du Pont and Jenkins stood by the fence to see how the pair hit it off. When the two horses began fighting for supremacy of their domain like two studs, Mrs. du Pont feared for Kelso's safety and screamed, "Get him out of there, Dickie. He's going to kill him." But Kelso stood his ground, and soon old Spray knew who was boss. From then on, the two became best friends, going out every day, with Mrs. du Pont on Kelso and Jenkins on Spray, or vice versa.

Even in retirement, Kelso continued receiving fan mail. Kelso's letters over the years probably reached well into the thousands. The good life continued. Charlie Potatoes had his buddy back and slept every night in Kelso's stall. While hacking around the Maryland countryside, Mrs. du Pont noticed that Kelso was very easy to handle and seemed to enjoy jumping small obstacles on the trail.

In the spring of 1967, Mrs. du Pont called Alison Cram, a former junior dressage champion living in Florida, and asked if she would be interested in teaching Kelso to become a show jumper. Cram was excited about the opportunity and flew up to Maryland. She began teaching Kelso in May, with the goal being to have him ready for a special appearance and demonstration at "National Steeplechase Day" at Saratoga on August 10. Kelso learned his lessons well and was sent to Saratoga, where he received a rousing ovation as he trotted and cantered before negotiating a four-jump course twice. He cleared six of the eight jumps cleanly. Tied to his forelock was the familiar yellow ribbon he had worn in most of his races.

Over the next few years Kelso continued to perform at different racetracks and competed at Madison Square Garden and other horse shows, winning a number of ribbons. At Woodstock he still hacked through the fields and was cared for by grooms Gene Moore and Junior Clevenger. But Kelso's real buddy was Pete, a former racehorse who had replaced Spray as his constant companion. Pete, whose real name was Sea Spirit, had won the New Jersey Futurity in 1961.

By 1974 Charlie Potatoes was getting old and suffered from a heart murmur, but he remained a loyal friend to Kelso. In July, Charlie was hit by a truck and killed. Kelso sulked for quite a while after Charlie's death. He hung his head and wouldn't eat with his usual enthusiasm. He was now seventeen, and although his back was beginning to sway a little and he had grown a bit of a belly, he still was as spry as a three-year-old.

Kelso continued to have visitors, and by now many of his loyal younger fans had children of their own.

Junior Clevenger would bring Kelso out and hear fathers and mothers say to their kids, "That's him; that's the horse I've always told you about."

Kelso always looked well-groomed for his visitors. Clevenger made sure all the mud was cleaned off of him and painted his feet with pine tar and mineral oil so they'd shine whenever people took pictures of him. Each morning when the sets of horses went to the training track, Kelso would watch them from his paddock, as if envious. He'd then go get Pete, and the two would go to the far end of the pasture where the ground was higher, giving them a good view of the training track. Kelso would stand motionless, watching the horses train. Another groom, Larry Schneiders, would watch him and think, "His body's here, but I sometimes think his heart's never left the track."

Final Farewell

I t was the early eighties, and Kelso was now well into his twenties. In the colder months he would wear his winter coat to keep him warm and walk a lot with Pete. He led a leisurely life, basically eating oats, hanging out with Pete, and watching the seasons roll by. The seventies had brought a new golden era to racing, as the elusive Triple Crown fell three times — to Secretariat, Seattle Slew, and Affirmed. Another grand gelding, named Forego, came along to capture the hearts of racing fans, followed in the early eighties by the rags-to-riches John Henry. The era of Kelso was slipping further into history.

Dickie Jenkins was long gone from Woodstock. He stayed another three years after Kelso's retirement, riding the old horse and fox hunting him, until a disagreement over a horse forced him to leave after seventeen years. After working as an assistant trainer at Fred Hooper's farm in Alabama, he began riding for a while up at Green Mountain racetrack in Vermont before taking on other jobs. He divorced his wife, with whom he had five children, and took a job at Cedar Lake Farm in Blairstown, New Jersey.

Carl Hanford and Mrs. du Pont parted company soon after Kelso's retirement. He trained for a few years after that before getting a job at the new Liberty Bell Racetrack (now Philadelphia Park), first as entry clerk, then steward. He subsequently worked as a steward at several tracks, including Garden State, Fair Grounds, Bowie, and Delaware Park.

Milo Valenzuela went on to be awarded the 1968 Kentucky Derby aboard Forward Pass after the disqualification of Dancer's Image, who tested positive for the then-illegal drug Butazolidin. He also won the 1974 Santa Anita Derby aboard Destroyer, as well as many other top races. He retired from the saddle in 1980 after winning only five races from 109 mounts that year.

Valenzuela tried his hand at training but just managed to eke out a living, training mainly at the California fair tracks. He gave it up in 1996 and became an assistant to trainer Fidel Cardiel. He outlived all his brothers, and of the twenty-one children and two adopted children, he and five of his sisters are the only survivors. Twelve of his brothers and sisters died at a young age, some at childbirth.

Milo's nephew, Patrick, has been one of the leading riders in the country for many years and achieved his greatest success winning the 1989 Kentucky Derby and Preakness aboard Sunday Silence and piloting the brilliant Arazi to a stunning victory in the 1991 Breeders' Cup Juvenile.

Now 68, Valenzuela suffers from diabetes, which afflicted many of his siblings. In September 2002, he suffered a stroke, then had two more strokes the following March.

His daughter, Diane, who works at Santa Anita, has been on a crusade to get her father elected to the Hall of Fame. But she knows she doesn't have much time, as Milo has told her, "If I don't get in while I'm alive, I want you to stop trying. I don't want to get in after I'm gone." Diane has also been looking into the possibility of doing a book about her father's life.

In the late sixties and early seventies, Mrs. du Pont

won major stakes with the top-class filly Politely and with King's Bishop, who broke Belmont's seven-furlong track record in the 1973 Carter Handicap.

Kelso's dam, Maid of Flight, never produced anything even remotely close to her famous first foal. After Kelso, Maid of Flight did produce eight other winners, including two stakes-placed horses: Pure Flight and T. V. Genie. The latter, who had finished third in a graded stakes at Monmouth Park, was the biggest money winner of this group with earnings of $63,996. Maid of Flight's filly named for Heather Noble managed only one victory in five starts.

In the early eighties Mrs. du Pont received several requests to send Kelso for public appearances. The old gelding had not been ridden for fourteen years, and Mrs. du Pont turned down all the requests. In 1983 she was contacted by Monique Koehler, president of the Thoroughbred Retirement Fund, asking if Mrs. du Pont would consider parading Kelso at Belmont Park on Jockey Club Gold Cup day, along with the other two grand geldings, Forego and John Henry. Forego was thirteen and residing at the Kentucky Horse Park, while John Henry still was racing at age eight and pointing for the Gold Cup. The three would lead the post parade for the big race. This time Mrs. du Pont did not turn down the request.

So, Kelso, at age twenty-six, prepared to return to Belmont Park for the first time in twenty-one years. First, a saddle was placed on his back, which he didn't seem to mind. Then, he was given a thorough examination by veterinarians, who said he physically was up to the trip. His condition was carefully monitored during dry runs. He had suffered a colic attack five years earlier, but when veterinarian Alan McCarthy examined him for a Coggins test (a blood test, necessary for travel, for the antibodies against the equine infectious anemia virus) four weeks before the trip to New York, he found the horse in excellent shape.

Kelso was put on a van on the morning of October 15, accompanied by his equine pal Pete and his groom Debby Ferguson. Mrs. du Pont had called Dickie Jenkins and asked him to be there. Despite their disagreement the two had remained close over the years. Jenkins was scheduled to be in Albany the next day, representing Cedar Lake Farm, to give a seminar on horse care and training. He figured he'd go to Belmont and then leave for Albany that night.

When Kelso arrived, he was taken out to graze and unwind. Jenkins showed up and noticed the horse was acting studdish. "Did you all give this horse a tranquilizer?" he asked Kelso's handlers. He was told that they had given him something to calm him down.

In the paddock before the Gold Cup, Kelso responded to the cheers of the crowd by bowing his neck in regal splendor. When Ferguson mounted and walked him around, she shouted to Mrs. du Pont, standing by the railing, "He's such a ham. Every time we come around he gets closer to the crowd."

As Kelso paraded around the paddock, memories of a similar scene some twenty years earlier overcame many in the crowd. The last they had seen of Kelso, the swaybacked, creaky old gelding had been a sleek racing machine decked out in yellow and gray — a vision embedded in their minds after so many unforgettable Saturdays.

Mrs. du Pont had Jenkins go over and have his picture taken with his old buddy. "You know, Mrs. du Pont, this old bugger is anxious as the git-go," Jenkins told her.

In the post parade Kelso was on his toes. After leading the parade with Forego and John Henry, he was brought back to the barn. Jenkins noticed he was sweating, and visions of all those hours spent holding intravenous bottles came back to him. "This ain't no good for this old son of a buck," he thought. "And him with tranquilizers in him." He bid his farewells to Kelso and headed up to Albany. The day had been a big success, as a crowd of more than 32,000 showed up and donated a total of $27,000 to the TRF. Unfortunately for John Henry, he could only manage a fifth-place finish in the Gold Cup, a race he had won in 1981 at age six.

Kelso was vanned back home later that night. The following morning, he was turned out in his paddock. He was checked at 11 a.m. and again at 2 p.m. by farm personnel and all seemed well. Later that afternoon some visitors arrived asking to see the horse, and when Mrs. du Pont led them to his paddock she noticed he appeared to be in some distress. He was brought to his stall, and Mrs. du Pont called Dr. McCarthy. When he examined Kelso, he found the horse was suffering from colic. He treated him with Banamine, an analgesic and anti-inflammatory drug, and with Jenotone, an anti-spasmodic and muscle relaxant.

The treatment seemed to help, and Kelso lay down, seemingly more relaxed. About forty-five minutes later, he got to his feet in apparent discomfort again. He began to tremble and his legs shook. There was nothing left to do but pray for a quick and merciful end. It came at 7 p.m. Two days earlier the once-familiar images of the racetrack and the sound of cheering crowds had been nothing more than a faint memory to the old horse. Now, with those images and sounds reborn and fresh in his mind, the Mighty Kelso bid his final farewell.

The next morning he was buried behind the office at Woodstock Farm with a simple ceremony. A devastated Mrs. du Pont remained in seclusion.

She continues to fly her Bohemia Stable colors, and over the years the majority of her horses have been trained by her old nemesis, Allen Jerkens. Together, they have had excellent success, sending out a number of graded stakes winners, such as Best of Luck, Dixie Flag, Dixie Luck, Shine Again, and Shiny Band.

Mrs. du Pont lost contact with Heather Noble over the years, but the *Kelsoland* newsletter continued to publish for more than ten years after his retirement, with the horse continuing to address his many fans and signing it, "Kelly-O."

As of 2003 Mrs. du Pont and Hanford still get together often for lunch and dinner. Hanford, 87, lives in Wilmington, Delaware, with Millie, his wife of forty-seven years. He was working as a steward at Delaware Park in 1990 when his daughter, Gail, took out her trainer's license, eventually bringing a string of horses to Delaware. Hanford felt it was a conflict of interest and retired from the sport for good. In 2003 Mrs. du Pont sent three horses to Gail, who had grown up with Kelso and sat on his back when she was two years old.

In 1987 Jenkins bought a forty-two-acre farm in Live Oak, Florida, where he lives with his second wife, with whom he had two more children. He takes care of six broodmares and three young horses, but was slowed down by a heart attack in 2002. He describes his home as a shrine to Kelso. But with most of his neighbors being pig farmers, he rarely gets a chance to reminisce about the old horse anymore.

Kelso has been dead for twenty years, yet his spirit still rules over Woodstock Farm, greeting all who enter its gates. Visitors cannot help but be aware of his presence as they drive along the white fence-lined roads and gaze upon the very ground over which he once galloped, and where he gallops still. Behind Mrs. duPont's office, Kelso's gravestone, surrounded by granite pillars, stands out like an historic monument.

The "Era of Kelso" is long gone, but the memories still are very much alive, especially for those who saw him race. There has never been a sight quite the equal of Kelso, with his familiar ribbon tied to his forelock and cumbersome weights piled on his once-scrawny frame. Still, he refused to yield to his burdens, gracing the racetrack with an elegance never before seen.

Kelso ruled his domain with an iron grip. His reign endured for seven long years and many wide-eyed young fans grew to adulthood during that time. He was many things to many people, but most of all, he was, as Shakespeare described Lear, "Every inch a king."

KELSO's
PEDIGREE

		Hyperion, 1930	Gainsborough Selene
	Alibhai, 1938		
YOUR HOST, ch, 1947		Teresina, 1920	Tracery Blue Tit
		Mahmoud, 1933	Blenheim II Mah Mahal
	Boudoir II, 1938		
KELSO, Dk. b/br. gelding, **1957**		Kampala, 1933	Clarissimus La Soupe II
		Reigh Count, 1925	Sunreigh Contessina
	Count Fleet, 1940		
MAID OF FLIGHT, br, 1951		Quickly, 1930	Haste Stephanie
		Man o' War, 1917	Fair Play Mahubah
	Maidoduntreath, 1939		
		Mid Victorian, 1932	Victorian Black Betty

KELSO's RACE RECORD

Kelso — **dkbbr. g. 1957, by Your Host (Alibhai)–Maid of Flight, by Count Fleet** — **Lifetime record: 63 39 12 2 $1,977,896**

Own.– Bohemia Stable
Br.– Mrs Richard C. duPont (Ky)
Tr.– C.H. Hanford

2Mar66- 9Hia	fst	6f	:22^2 :44^4 1:10	4↑ Alw 10000	8	3	$8^{7\frac34}$	$8^{9\frac34}$	$7^{7\frac34}$	$4^{4\frac12}$	Boland W	113	3.30	89-13	DavusII119^{hd}TimeTested119^{1}CountryFrind113$^{3\frac12}$	Closed well	8
22Sep65- 7Aqu	fst	1¼	:47^3 1:12 1:36^4 2:02^4	3↑ Stymie H 27k	6	4	$4^{5\frac12}$	$1^{\frac12}$	1^6	1^8	Valenzuela I	128	*.30	84-17	Kelso128^8[D]O'Har107$^{\frac34}$Ky.Ponr110$^{\frac34}$	With complete authority	6
6Sep65- 7Aqu	fst	1⅛	:48^1 1:12^1 1:36^3 1:49	3↑ Aqueduct 108k	7	5	5^{10}	5^6	4^8	4^9	Valenzuela I	130	*1.00	82-14	Malicious116^{3}Pluck116^{no}RmnBrothr121^6	Lacked any response	7
7Aug65- 6Sar	fst	1⅛	:47^1 1:11^1 1:36^4 1:49^4	4↑ Whitney 54k	3	4	4^4	4^5	$2^{2\frac12}$	1no	Valenzuela I	130	*1.20	96-08	Kelso130^{no}Malicious114^{6}PiaStar127^{nk}	Up in final strides	5
24Jly65- 7Aqu	fst	1¼	:47 1:10^2 1:35 2:00^3	3↑ Brooklyn H 107k	1	5	$5^{6\frac12}$	$4^{3\frac12}$	$3^{3\frac12}$	3^4	Valenzuela I	132	*1.20	91-10	PiaStar121^{2}RomnBrothr121^{2}Kelso132$^{1\frac12}$	Hung under impost	5
10Jly65- 8Del	fst	1$\frac{1}{16}$	:24^1 :48^2 1:12^2 1:42^2	3↑ Diamond State H 21k	2	2	$2^{1\frac12}$	$2^{\frac12}$	$1^{\frac12}$	$1^{3\frac14}$	Valenzuela I	130	*.30	97-13	Kelso130$^{3\frac14}$Kilmoray109^{3}Big Brigade114^{no}	Going away	4
29Jun65- 8Mth	fst	6f	:22^2 :45^4 1:11^1	4↑ Alw 5000	8	3	5^6	$8^{6\frac34}$	$5^{4\frac14}$	$3^{\frac12}$	Boland W	122	*.50	85-23	Cachto117^{no}Communqu122$^{\frac12}$Klso122^{hd}	Showed strong late bid	8
11Nov64- 7Lrl	hd	1½Ⓣ	:46^4 1:10^2 2:00 2:23^4	3↑ D C Int'l 150k	5	2	2^4	$1^{\frac12}$	1^3	$1^{4\frac12}$	Valenzuela I	126	*1.20	112-00	Kelso126$^{4\frac12}$Gun Bow126^{9}Aniline122$^{3\frac12}$	Drew out handily	8
31Oct64- 7Aqu	fst	2	:48^4 2:53^3 3:19^1	3↑ J C Gold Cup 108k	2	5	4^3	$1^{1\frac12}$	1^4	$1^{5\frac12}$	Valenzuela I	124	*.45	101-14	Kelso124$^{5\frac12}$Roman Brother119^{6}Quadrangle119^{16}	Easy score	6
3Oct64- 7Aqu	gd	1¼	:48^1 1:12^1 1:37^1 2:02^2	3↑ Woodward 108k	3	2	$2^{1\frac12}$	2^{hd}	1^{hd}	2no	Valenzuela I	126	*.95	86-22	Gun Bow126^{no}Kelso126^{4}Quadrangle121^{25}	Bore in slightly	5
7Sep64- 7Aqu	fst	1⅛	:46^3 1:10^4 1:35^3 1:48^3	3↑ Aqueduct 107k	3	2	2^5	$2^{1\frac12}$	$1^{\frac12}$	$1^{\frac34}$	Valenzuela I	128	2.20	98-16	Klso128$^{\frac34}$GnBow128^{6}Sadm119$^{4\frac12}$	Responded to strong urging	5
27Aug64- 7Sar	hd	1⅛Ⓣ	1:46^3	3↑ Alw 9500	4	2	$2^{2\frac12}$	2^{hd}	$1^{\frac12}$	$1^{2\frac12}$	Valenzuela I	118	*.30	102-00	Klso118$^{2\frac12}$Knghtsboro116$^{1\frac12}$RockyThumb120^5	Scored in hand	8
25Jly64- 7Aqu	fst	1¼	:46^1 1:10^1 1:35 1:59^3	3↑ Brooklyn H 110k	5	6	6^9	$5^{8\frac12}$	6^{10}	5^{14}	Valenzuela I	130	*.85	88-12	GnBow122^{12}OldnTimes122^{no}SunriseFlght113^{hd}	Bumped gate	8
18Jly64- 8Mth	fst	1¼	:45^1 1:10^1 1:35^3 2:01^4	3↑ Monmouth H 107k	1	5	5^6	$4^{3\frac14}$	$3^{\frac12}$	2^{nk}	Valenzuela I	130	*.60	93-17	Mngo127^{nk}Klso130$^{4\frac12}$GunBow124^{18}	Hung through late stages	5
4Jly64- 7Aqu	fst	1¼	:47^2 1:11^2 1:36^4 2:01^4	3↑ Suburban H 110k	6	4	3^4	3^2	$3^{1\frac12}$	2^{hd}	Valenzuela I	131	*1.35	91-17	Iron Peg116^{hd}Kelso131^{4}Olden Times128$^{\frac34}$	Getting to winner	8
25Jun64- 7Aqu	fst	1⅛	:48^3 1:12^4 1:37^1 1:50	3↑ Handicap 15000	5	4	$4^{3\frac12}$	$2^{1\frac12}$	$1^{1\frac12}$	$1^{1\frac14}$	Valenzuela I	136	*.55	91-15	Kelso136$^{1\frac14}$TropicalBreeze114$^{\frac12}$SunrisFlght121^{10}	Mild drive	5
6Jun64- 8Hol	fst	1$\frac{1}{16}$	:22^4 :46^1 1:10^2 1:41^3	3↑ Californian 115k	3	5	6^5	$7^{5\frac14}$	$7^{8\frac34}$	6^8	Valenzuela I	127	*1.40	79-14	Mustard Plaster111$^{1\frac12}$Mr. Consistency123$^{1\frac12}$ColordoKing123$^{2\frac12}$	Impeded	10
23May64- 8Hol	fst	7f	:21^4 :44 1:08^4 1:21^2	3↑ Los Angeles H 55k	9	1	7^{13}	$9^{8\frac12}$	9^{13}	$8^{9\frac14}$	Valenzuela I	130	*1.70	84-13	Cyrano124^{hd}QuitaDude114^{2}Admiral'sVoyag121^{no}	Dull effort	9
11Nov63- 7Lrl	fm	1½Ⓣ	:48^3 1:13^3 2:03^3 2:27^2	3↑ D C Int'l 150k	8	4	$4^{1\frac12}$	2^1	$2^{\frac12}$	$2^{\frac12}$	Valenzuela I	126	*.50	93-14	Mongo126$^{\frac12}$Klso126^{12}Nyrcos122^3	Sluggish start,game effort	10
19Oct63- 7Aqu	fst	2	:48^2 2:30 2:55^1 3:22	3↑ J C Gold Cup 108k	1	4	2^{hd}	1^2	1^6	1^4	Valenzuela I	124	*.15	87-14	Kelso124^{4}Guadalcanal124^{5}Garwol124$^{3\frac12}$	Speed in reserve	7
28Sep63- 7Aqu	fst	1¼	:47^3 1:11^4 1:36^2 2:00^4	3↑ Woodward 108k	2	3	3^4	$2^{\frac12}$	$1^{\frac12}$	$1^{3\frac12}$	Valenzuela I	126	*.25	96-13	Kelso126$^{3\frac12}$NeverBend120$^{1\frac12}$CrimsonSatn126^6	Speed to spare	5
2Sep63- 7Aqu	fst	1⅛	:49 1:12^4 1:37^1 1:49^4	3↑ Aqueduct 110k	7	3	$4^{1\frac12}$	3^1	1^2	$1^{5\frac12}$	Valenzuela I	134	*.70	92-17	Kelso134$^{5\frac12}$CrimsonSatan129^{hd}Grwol116^{no}	Under mild urging	8
3Aug63- 6Sar	fst	1⅛	:48 1:12 1:37^2 1:50^2	4↑ Whitney 55k	2	4	$4^{2\frac12}$	$4^{2\frac12}$	1^1	$1^{2\frac12}$	Valenzuela I	130	*.35	93-14	Kelso130$^{2\frac12}$Saidam111^{1}Sunrise County117^{hd}	Easily the best	7
4Jly63- 7Aqu	fst	1¼	:48^4 1:13^1 1:38^1 2:01^4	3↑ Suburban H 108k	7	3	3^3	$3^{1\frac12}$	$1^{1\frac12}$	$1^{1\frac14}$	Valenzuela I	133	*.45	91-13	Kelso133$^{1\frac14}$Saidam111$^{1\frac12}$Garwol112^1	Retained a safe margin	7
19Jun63- 7Aqu	fst	1⅛	:47^4 1:11^3 1:36 1:48^4	3↑ Nassau County 27k	3	3	$3^{1\frac12}$	3^1	1^2	$1^{1\frac12}$	Valenzuela I	132	*.30	97-07	Kelso132$^{1\frac12}$Lnvn114^{no}Polyld114^3	Cleverly rated,easy score	5
23Mar63- 8Bow	fst	1$\frac{1}{16}$	:24^2 :48^1 1:12 1:43	3↑ J B Campbell H 109k	5	5	$4^{4\frac12}$	3^3	$2^{1\frac12}$	$1^{\frac34}$	Valenzuela I	131	*.80	98-15	Kelso131$^{\frac34}$Crimson Satan124^{hd}Gushing Wind116^6	Hard drive	6
16Mar63- 8GP	fst	1¼	:48^2 1:12^1 1:37^2 2:03^1	3↑ Gulf Park H 110k	2	2	$1^{\frac12}$	1^2	1^2	$1^{3\frac14}$	Valenzuela I	130	*.20	83-20	Kelso130$^{3\frac14}$Sensitivo112^{9}Jay Fox113$^{\frac12}$	Speed in reserve	6
23Feb63- 7Hia	fst	1¼	:48^3 1:12^2 1:36^4 2:01^4	3↑ Widener H 128k	5	3	$5^{4\frac12}$	$4^{2\frac12}$	2^3	$2^{2\frac14}$	Valenzuela I	131	*.45	87-18	Beau Purple125$^{2\frac14}$Kelso131^{3}Heroshogala110^4	Best of others	9
9Feb63- 7Hia	fst	1⅛	:46^2 1:10^4 1:35^4 1:48^4	3↑ Seminole H 58k	1	4	$4^{7\frac12}$	4^2	1^2	$1^{2\frac34}$	Valenzuela I	128	2.35	91-19	Kelso128$^{2\frac34}$Ridan129$^{2\frac12}$Senstvo115$^{3\frac12}$	Rallied wide,drew away	6
30Jan63- 8Hia	fst	7f	:23^3 :46 1:10^1 1:22^4	3↑ Palm Beach H 29k	4	2	2^{hd}	3^2	$4^{3\frac12}$	$4^{5\frac12}$	Valenzuela I	128	2.45	89-16	Ridan127$^{3\frac34}$Jaipur127$^{\frac34}$MerryRulr117^1	Broke in stride,tired	5
1Dec62- 8GS	fst	1½	:49^3 1:15 2:05^1 2:30^1	3↑ Gov's Plate 54k	2	1	1^{hd}	1^3	1^3	1^5	Valenzuela I	129	*.40	105-20	Kelso129^{5}Bass Clef117^{5}Polylad117^8	Drew away with ease	5

KELSO's **RACE RECORD** CONTINUED

12Nov62- 7Lrl	sf	1½Ⓣ	:47^{1} 1:11^{2} 2:03^{1} 2:28^{1}	3↑ D C Int'l 125k	3	2	2^{hd}	1^{1}	1^{hd}	$2^{1\frac{1}{2}}$	Valenzuela I	126	2.10	88-20	MatchII128$^{1\frac{1}{2}}$Kelso126$^{4\frac{1}{2}}$CarryBack126^{5}	Easily best of rest	13
27Oct62- 7Bel	sf	1½Ⓣ	2:28^{3}	3↑ Man o' War 114k	12	5	4^{3}	$2^{1\frac{1}{2}}$	2^{2}	2^{2}	Valenzuela I	126	*1.05	101-11	BeauPurple126^{2}Klso126$^{6\frac{1}{2}}$ThAxII126$^{1\frac{1}{4}}$	Finished very gamely	12
20Oct62- 7Bel	fst	2	:48^{3} 2:28^{2} 2:53^{2} 3:19^{4}	3↑ J C Gold Cup 108k	3	2	3^{2}	1^{2}	1^{8}	1^{10}	Valenzuela I	124	*.25	103-08	Kelso124^{10}Guadalcanal124^{2}Nickel Boy124$^{1\frac{1}{2}}$	Easily best	6
29Sep62- 7Aqu	gd	1¼	:47^{1} 1:11^{3} 1:37 2:03^{1}	3↑ Woodward 115k	5	3	$3^{8\frac{1}{2}}$	1^{3}	1^{3}	$1^{4\frac{1}{2}}$	Valenzuela I	126	*.90	84-17	Kelso126$^{4\frac{1}{2}}$Jaipur120$^{6\frac{1}{2}}$Guadlcnl126$^{1\frac{1}{2}}$	Won as rider pleased	8
19Sep62- 7Aqu	fst	1¼	:48 1:12 1:36^{2} 2:00^{4}	3↑ Stymie H 29k	2	3	$3^{4\frac{1}{2}}$	$1^{1\frac{1}{2}}$	1^{3}	$1^{2\frac{1}{2}}$	Valenzuela I	128	*1.25	96-14	Klso128$^{2\frac{1}{2}}$Plyld114^{hd}Tutnkhmn110^{hd}	With complete authority	11
8Sep62- 7Atl	fm	1$\frac{1}{16}$Ⓣ	1:43^{1}	3↑ Alw 6000	2	1	2^{hd}	$1^{1\frac{1}{2}}$	$1^{\frac{1}{2}}$	$4^{1\frac{3}{4}}$	Pierce D	113	*.40	93-05	CalltheWitness113^{nk}ArtMarket113^{hd}WindySands113$^{1\frac{1}{2}}$	Tired	7
22Aug62- 6Sar	fm	1$\frac{1}{16}$Ⓣ	1:41^{4}	3↑ Alw 5000	3	4	$4^{1\frac{3}{4}}$	$2^{\frac{1}{2}}$	$1^{\frac{1}{2}}$	$1^{1\frac{1}{2}}$	Valenzuela I	124	*.25	97-03	Kelso124$^{1\frac{1}{2}}$CalltheWitness117^{5}FountainHill117^{2}	Mild drive	7
14Jly62- 8Mth	fst	1¼	:46 1:10 1:34^{4} 2:00^{2}	3↑ Monmouth H 109k	5	4	$4^{5\frac{1}{2}}$	4^{4}	$4^{2\frac{1}{2}}$	2^{3}	Shoemaker W	130	*.80	101-14	Carry Back124^{3}Kelso130$^{\frac{3}{4}}$Beau Purple117$^{\frac{1}{2}}$	In close turn	6
4Jly62- 7Aqu	fst	1¼	:48^{4} 1:12^{4} 1:36^{3} 2:00^{3}	3↑ Suburban H 105k	4	3	3^{6}	2^{2}	2^{2}	$2^{2\frac{1}{2}}$	Shoemaker W	132	*.65	100-08	BeauPurpl115$^{2\frac{1}{2}}$Klso132$^{3\frac{1}{2}}$Grwol109$^{1\frac{1}{4}}$	Couldn't reach winner	4
16Jun62- 3Bel	fst	1	:24^{1} :47^{2} 1:11^{3} 1:35^{3}	3↑ Alw 7500	2	4	4^{2}	2^{2}	2^{hd}	$1^{2\frac{1}{4}}$	Shoemaker W	117	*.25	96-14	Klso117$^{2\frac{1}{4}}$Grwol115$^{3\frac{1}{2}}$RosNt117$^{\frac{1}{2}}$	Rated early,drew out easily	6
30May62- 7Aqu	fst	1	:22^{1} :44 1:08 1:33^{3}	3↑ Metropolitan H 111k	2	6	6^{9}	$5^{6\frac{1}{2}}$	5^{10}	$6^{8\frac{1}{4}}$	Shoemaker W	133	*.60	92-08	CarryBack123$^{2\frac{1}{2}}$MerryRuler120$^{\frac{1}{2}}$RullahRed111$^{4\frac{1}{2}}$	Dull effort	9
11Nov61- 7Lrl	fm	1½Ⓣ	:48^{3} 2:01^{3} 2:26^{1}	3↑ D C Int'l 100k	6	1	$1^{\frac{1}{2}}$	1^{hd}	2^{hd}	$2^{\frac{3}{4}}$	Arcaro E	126	*.40	108-01	T.V.Lrk126$^{\frac{3}{4}}$Klso126^{12}Prnupcl126^{10}	Made very sharp effort	8
21Oct61- 7Aqu	fst	2	:49^{4} 2:35 3:00^{4} 3:25^{4}	3↑ J C Gold Cup 105k	3	2	2^{2}	1^{3}	1^{4}	1^{5}	Arcaro E	124	*.10	68-25	Kelso124^{5}Hillsborough124^{8}Peace Isle124^{30}	Easily best	4
30Sep61- 7Bel	fst	1¼	:46^{1} 1:10 1:34^{4} 2:00	3↑ Woodward 109k	5	3	$2^{1\frac{1}{2}}$	2^{hd}	1^{3}	1^{8}	Arcaro E	126	*.50	100-13	Kelso126^{8}Divine Comedy126$^{\frac{1}{2}}$Carry Back120^{nk}	Much the best	5
4Sep61- 8AP	gd	1	:22^{4} :45^{2} 1:09^{3} 1:34^{3}	3↑ Wash Park H 120k	8	9	$10^{6\frac{1}{2}}$	6^{7}	4^{7}	$4^{5\frac{3}{4}}$	Arcaro E	132	*.70	94-08	ChiefofChiefs112$^{4\frac{3}{4}}$TalentShow110^{nk}RunforNurse112$^{\frac{3}{4}}$	Boxed	11
22Jly61- 7Aqu	fst	1¼	:46^{2} 1:10^{1} 1:36 2:01^{3}	3↑ Brooklyn H 112k	7	4	3^{16}	$3^{5\frac{1}{2}}$	$3^{1\frac{1}{2}}$	$1^{1\frac{1}{4}}$	Arcaro E	136	*.50	98-10	Klso136$^{1\frac{1}{4}}$DvnComdy118^{no}Yorky122^{hd}	Under strong handling	10
4Jly61- 7Aqu	fst	1¼	:48^{2} 1:12^{2} 1:37^{3} 2:02	3↑ Suburban H 111k	7	4	$4^{3\frac{1}{2}}$	3^{nk}	1^{2}	1^{5}	Arcaro E	133	*.60	96-13	Kelso133^{5}NickelBoy112^{nk}TalentShow110^{hd}	Speed in reserve	10
17Jun61- 7Bel	fst	1⅛	:45^{4} 1:10^{2} 1:35^{1} 1:48	4↑ Whitney 56k	5	3	$3^{3\frac{1}{2}}$	1^{1}	2^{hd}	2^{hd}	Arcaro E	130	*.45	96-12	DOur Hope111^{hd}Kelso130^{5}Reinzi114^{hd}	Roughed repeatedly	7
	Placed first through disqualification																
30May61- 7Aqu	fst	1	:23 :46 1:10^{2} 1:35^{3}	3↑ Metropolitan H 114k	9	8	$8^{5\frac{1}{4}}$	$7^{6\frac{1}{4}}$	4^{4}	1^{nk}	Arcaro E	130	*1.05	90-16	Kelso130^{nk}AllHands117^{3}SweetWillim108^{4}	Altered course,up	10
19May61- 7Aqu	fst	7f	:23 :46^{1} 1:11 1:24	4↑ Alw 10000	7	6	$5^{4\frac{1}{2}}$	$3^{1\frac{1}{2}}$	2^{hd}	$1^{1\frac{1}{2}}$	Arcaro E	124	*.35	90-17	Kelso124$^{1\frac{1}{2}}$Gyro115^{nk}LongGoneJohn121$^{\frac{1}{2}}$	Drew out with ease	8
29Oct60- 7Aqu	sly	2	:47^{2} 2:29 2:54 3:19^{2}	3↑ J C Gold Cup 109k	8	3	3^{13}	$2^{\frac{1}{2}}$	1^{1}	$1^{3\frac{1}{2}}$	Arcaro E	119	*.80	114-16	Kelso119$^{3\frac{1}{2}}$Don Poggio124^{10}Bald Eagle124^{15}	Speed to spare	8
15Oct60- 8Haw	my	1¼	:46^{4} 1:11^{3} 1:36^{4} 2:02	3↑ Haw Gold Cup H 144k	4	6	$4^{1\frac{1}{2}}$	1^{2}	1^{3}	1^{6}	Arcaro E	117	*2.20	86-21	Kelso117^{6}Heroshogala119$^{\frac{1}{2}}$On-and-On122$^{1\frac{3}{4}}$	Speed to spare	9
28Sep60- 7Bel	fst	1⅝	:47^{2} 1:37^{2} 2:02^{1} 2:40^{4}	Lawrence Realizatn 56k	1	4	$4^{2\frac{1}{2}}$	1^{1}	1^{4}	$1^{4\frac{1}{2}}$	Arcaro E	120	*.50	100-14	Kelso120$^{4\frac{1}{2}}$Tompion123$^{1\frac{1}{2}}$ToothandNal116$^{5\frac{1}{2}}$	Speed in reserve	8
14Sep60- 7Aqu	fst	1⅛	:46^{3} 1:10^{2} 1:35^{4} 1:48^{2}	Discovery H 28k	2	6	$4^{3\frac{1}{2}}$	4^{2}	$1^{\frac{1}{2}}$	$1^{1\frac{1}{4}}$	Arcaro E	124	*1.20	102-14	Kelso124$^{1\frac{1}{4}}$CarelssJohn116$^{1\frac{1}{2}}$CountAmbr116$^{\frac{1}{2}}$	Swerved,driving	8
3Sep60- 7Aqu	fst	1	:22^{3} :45^{2} 1:10 1:34^{4}	Jerome H 59k	7	9	$9^{5\frac{1}{4}}$	5^{3}	$3^{2\frac{1}{2}}$	1^{hd}	Arcaro E	121	2.65	94-13	Kelso121^{hd}CarelessJohn116$^{2\frac{1}{2}}$FourLan119$^{2\frac{1}{2}}$	Long,hard drive	13
3Aug60- 7Mth	fst	1$\frac{1}{16}$	:22^{4} :46 1:09^{3} 1:41^{1}	Choice 56k	7	2	2^{1}	1^{1}	1^{6}	1^{7}	Hartack W	114	3.90	99-18	Klso114^{7}CarelessJohn114$^{\frac{3}{4}}$CountAmber114$^{3\frac{1}{2}}$	Speed to spare	8
23Jly60- 8AP	fst	1	:22^{3} :45^{2} 1:10^{3} 1:36^{1}	Arl Classic 135k	5	10	$7^{5\frac{1}{4}}$	$9^{7\frac{3}{4}}$	$7^{7\frac{1}{2}}$	$8^{7\frac{1}{2}}$	Brooks S	117	3.90	81-13	T.V. Lark120$^{\frac{3}{4}}$John William123$^{2\frac{1}{2}}$Venetian Way123^{1}	Dull try	12
16Jly60- 5Aqu	fst	1	:23 :45^{1} 1:09 1:34^{1}	Alw 4500	4	1	$1^{\frac{1}{2}}$	1^{3}	1^{10}	1^{12}	Blum W	117	*1.30	97-10	Kelso117^{12}DoubleDly120^{no}AugustSun109^{nk}	As rider pleased	8
22Jun60- 5Mth	fst	6f	:21^{4} :45 1:10	Alw 4500	6	3	$4^{3\frac{1}{2}}$	3^{1}	1^{3}	1^{10}	Hartack W	117	*1.00	92-12	Kelso117^{10}Burnt Clover117$^{2\frac{1}{2}}$Gordian Knot117$^{1\frac{1}{2}}$	Ridden out	8
	Previously trained by J.M. Lee																
23Sep59- 3Atl	fst	7f	:22 :44^{2} 1:09^{3} 1:23	©Alw 3600	3	5	2^{hd}	1^{hd}	2^{hd}	$2^{\frac{3}{4}}$	Blum W	117	*1.90	87-11	WindySands117$^{\frac{3}{4}}$Klso117^{2}WeGuarantee117$^{2\frac{1}{2}}$	Made good try	8
14Sep59- 4Atl	fst	6f	:23^{1} :46^{2} 1:11^{2}	©Alw 3400	6	4	$4^{2\frac{1}{4}}$	$4^{2\frac{1}{2}}$	$4^{3\frac{1}{2}}$	$2^{1\frac{1}{2}}$	Block J	117	4.40	86-18	DressUp120$^{1\frac{1}{2}}$Kelso117$^{1\frac{3}{4}}$DuskyRam117^{nk}	Rallied for placing	7
4Sep59- 2Atl	gd	6f	:23^{2} :47^{1} 1:13^{4}	©Md Sp Wt	7	8	$7^{2\frac{1}{4}}$	6^{6}	4^{5}	$1^{1\frac{1}{4}}$	Block J	120	6.00	76-23	Kelso120$^{1\frac{1}{4}}$Crafty Master120$^{\frac{3}{4}}$Adapt120^{1}	Under a hard drive	12

Index

Aiken, S.C. 76-77, 96, 98, 120

Aiken Trials...76

Alibhai 16

Ambehaving 52

Aqueduct................52-53, 58-59, 61-62, 72, 102, 107, 112-113, 124, 139,
141, 143, 155-156, 159, 161-162, 165, 181

Aqueduct Handicap 72, 155

Arcaro, Eddie...........43, 62-64, 70-71, 73-74, 79, 81-82, 84, 86-89, 92-97,
99, 111-112, 173

Armstrong, F. Wallis 18

Bald Eagle 59, 64, 71, 73-74

Bally Ache..43

Beau Purple.......103-108, 113-117, 127, 129-133, 143-144, 146, 163, 176

Belmont.................24, 42-43, 57, 61, 64, 72, 79, 82, 87, 92, 100, 109, 114,
137, 141, 143, 161, 164-165, 191-192

Block, Henry..31

Block, John..30, 32

Blum, Walter 32, 58, 61, 158, 170

Bohemia Stable 22, 41, 51, 168, 195

Boudoir II 16

Brooklyn Handicap....................66, 80, 86, 88, 90, 140-141, 154, 156, 177

Brooks, Steve 59-60, 129

Candy Spots..141

Carry Back 78-79, 92-93, 100, 104, 106-109, 115-118, 127, 135, 142-144

Charlie Potatoes (dog) 121, 137, 175, 185-186

Circle S Ranch 17

Claiborne Farm..12, 20, 52, 175

Clevenger, Junior 186-187

colic 30, 120, 155, 181, 192, 194

Count Fleet..13, 93

Cram, Alison...185

Crimson Satan 127, 135-136, 141-144

Don Poggio...72-74, 85, 87

Dotted Swiss 64, 72

Dreyfus, Jack 102-104, 130-134

Duntreath Farm...13

du Pont, Allaire 12, 14, 18, 20-22, 24-26, 28-35, 40-43, 45-46, 48-56,
        61, 72-75, 78, 84, 114, 120-121, 125, 134-138, 149-151, 157-158,
           160, 163, 167-169, 171-173, 175-176, 182, 184-185, 189-196

du Pont, Lana 49, 169, 172

du Pont, Richard C. 49

Edwards, James 14

Everett, Mrs. Kelso 26

Finney, Humphrey S. 17

Fitzpatrick, Lawrence "Fitz" 98

Forego 35, 93, 133, 188, 191, 194

"Giant Killer"...102, 133

gliders 49-50

Goetz, William 14

Gratton, J.U. 40

Greek Money..99

Gun Bow.....................................58, 154, 156-159, 161-164, 167-171, 174

Hallahan, Jimmy 25, 35, 52

Hall, Billy...66, 90, 98

Hancock, A.B. Jr. 21, 45, 52, 175

Handicap Triple Crown 79-80, 86, 90

Hanford, Carl 34-37, 39-41, 44-46, 56-62, 64, 68-69, 72-75, 78-79, 82,
        84, 86, 88, 90-91, 94-95, 98-101, 108-110, 114-116, 118, 131-132,
     134-140, 146, 149-152, 155, 157, 163, 167, 175-176, 180, 183, 189, 196

Hanford, Ira "Babe" 37-40, 59, 68-70

Hartack, Bill 43, 57, 61-62

Harthill, Alex 45, 183

Heroshogala 67-68, 71

Horse of the Year 49, 57, 65, 71-72, 75, 78, 81-82, 96, 98, 119, 132,
147, 149, 163-164, 167, 172, 174, 180-182

Hyperion 13, 16

Iron Peg 153-154

Jaipur 109-110, 112-113, 127-129

Jenkins, Dick 18-19, 22-30, 41-45, 52-53, 62-63, 66-67, 80-81, 84, 86,
90-92, 105, 108-110, 112, 127-128, 134-135, 149-153, 155, 164-165,
167, 178-185, 188, 192-194, 196

Jerkens, Allen 102-105, 114-115, 130-134, 195

Jockey Club Gold Cup 65, 71-72, 85, 93, 142, 144, 163-164, 166, 191

John Henry 188, 191, 194

Johnson, P.G. 67-71, 179

Kelso 12, 14, 22, 25-34, 41-46, 49, 51-71, 74-102, 104-108, 110-118,
120-126, 128-147, 149-189, 191-197

Kelso Fan Club 124, 177

Kelsoland 120, 122, 124-126, 128, 144, 177, 195

Kilmoray 131-132

Kulina, Bobby 83

Kulina, Joe 77, 83

LaBoyne, Bones 62

Lee, Dr. John 28-29, 32, 34, 66

Lloyd's of London 16

Longden, Johnny 15, 94, 96

Mahmoud 13, 16

Maid of Flight 12-14, 18-21, 26, 28, 31, 191

Maidoduntreath 13

Malicious 178, 180-181

Man o' War 13, 65, 72, 77, 114-115, 163

Maryland 21, 35, 37, 48-49, 53-54, 66, 99, 127, 135, 185

Mason, Mrs. Silas 13

Match II..116-118

McCarthy, Alan...192

Metropolitan Handicap.....................59, 72, 79, 85, 99, 137, 139, 153, 180

Moore, Gene..186

Mongo.............................116, 127, 135-136, 140, 142, 145-146, 154, 163

Monmouth Handicap..87, 107, 110, 140, 154

Neloy, Eddie..156, 163

Nerud, John..42

Never Bend..142-144

Noble, Heather.............................122-125, 168, 171, 173, 177, 191, 195

Olden Times...154

Our Hope..83-84, 87

Panamerica..51

Parke, Burley...41, 65

Pete (pony)..121, 186-188, 192

Pia Star...177-178, 180-181

Price, Jack...78, 109, 142

Quadrangle...161-162, 164-165, 177

Radnor Hunt Club..48

Ridan...99, 109, 127-129

Riddle, Samuel...13

Roman Brother..164-166, 177, 181-182

Rooney, Art...40, 46

Rosenberger, George..29

Sager, Colonel Floyd...20

Sharp, Bayard...22, 52

Sherluck..79

Shoemaker, Bill.....................92, 99-100, 106-107, 110, 141, 143

show jumper...185

Sir Gaylord..99

soaring records..51

Spray (pony) 121, 184-186

Stephens, Woody...72, 76, 142, 153

Stewart, "Irish Jimmy" 35, 39

Suburban Handicap..........80, 84-85, 92, 101-102, 104-106, 115-116, 139, 153, 177

Taylor, Edward P. 54

The Axe II...115-116

Thoroughbred Retirement Fund 191

Tom Fool 80, 85-86

Tompion 43, 46, 61-65, 92

Trotter, Tommy 36-37, 77-80, 84-87, 89, 92-93, 100-101, 104, 152-153

T. V. Lark..60, 64-65, 94-96, 113, 115

Valenzuela, Ismael "Milo" 110-113, 115-118, 129, 132-134, 139-140, 143-146, 152, 155, 157-158, 160-162, 166, 169-171, 176, 180, 189-190

Venetian Way 43, 46, 57, 60

Washington, D.C., International.....49, 72, 74, 93, 116, 127, 130, 145, 163

Whisk Broom II 80, 93

Whitney Handicap 65, 82, 84, 140, 156, 160, 178

Widener Handicap 71, 87, 109, 112, 127-131, 180

Woodstock Farm 21-22, 34, 41, 49, 51-52, 54, 120, 137, 174, 182, 184, 186, 188, 195-196

Woodward Handicap 64, 72, 92, 112, 136, 142-144, 161

Your Host 12, 14-18, 26, 41

Photo Credits

ABOUT THE
AUTHOR

S teve Haskin has been national correspondent for *Daily Racing Form* and senior correspondent for *The Blood-Horse* and provided lead coverage of the Triple Crown for more than twenty years; he now covers the Triple Crown for Secretariat.com. His weekly Derby Dozen and Kentucky Derby Rankings have been a fixture in *The Blood-Horse* and Secretariat.com for a quarter of a century. He also is the author of numerous books, including *Horse Racing's Holy Grail: The Epic Quest for the Kentucky Derby* and profiles of the racehorses Kelso, Dr. Fager, and John Henry. Haskin has won numerous awards for his writing and career achievement, and was elected to the National Museum of Racing and Hall of Fame's Media Roll of Honor in 2016. He lives in Rocky Hill, Connecticut.